MEMORY FOR ACTIONS

Memory for Actions

Johannes Engelkamp
Department of Psychology
University of the Saarland
Saarbrücken, Germany

Psychology Press
a member of the Taylor & Francis group

Copyright © 1998 by Psychology Press Ltd.,
a member of the Taylor & Francis group
   All rights reserved. No part of this book may be reproduced in any
   form, by photostat, microform, retrieval system, or any other
   means without the prior written permission of the publisher.

Psychology Press, Publishers
27 Church Road
Hove
East Sussex, BN3 2FA
UK

British Library Cataloguing in Publication Data

A catalogue record for this book is available from the British Library.

   ISBN 0-86377-765-1
   ISSN 0959-4779

Typeset by DP Photosetting, Aylesbury, Bucks.
Printed and bound in the United Kingdom by Biddles Ltd.,
Guildford and King's Lynn

Contents

Preface

Remembering what we have done, what we have seen others doing, and what we have been told that others have done is a basic requirement of everyday cognition. This book deals with the memory mechanisms that enable us to achieve this everyday cognition. This essay will focus on the observation that our memory for self-performed actions is particularly good. It will be argued that the processes of action planning and execution are decisive for this good memory performance. Many findings in the field of remembering self-performed actions can be derived from features characteristic of these two processes. Little attention has been paid to our memory of action events and to the role of output processes for memory in general; this essay presents an attempt to overcome this deficit. Besides presenting an explanation of the findings observed in the field of remembering self-performed actions, the book gives an almost comprehensive overview of the studies in this field published to date.

This essay is a strongly shortened version of a German book entitled *Das Erinnern eigener Handlungen*, which was published in 1997 by Hogrefe in Göttingen. The writing was supported by the German Science Foundation (DFG, Em 124/13).

I am grateful to Cheryl Lobb de Rahman for helping with the preparation of the English version of the text, and to Uta Plisch for having prepared the final form of the text. Finally, I am grateful for the indulgence of my wife while I was working on the English version of this book.

J. Engelkamp
Saarbrücken, July 1997

CHAPTER ONE

Introduction

Questions such as "Did you already get some petrol?", "Have you posted the letter?", and so on are, as a rule, able to be answered without difficulty. In other words, we remember our own actions well and this is without doubt highly important. Imagine you forgot that you had just put petrol in the car and immediately drove into the next petrol station to fill up again. Or that you forgot that you had paid the waiter in a restaurant and tried to pay again, or that you forgot you had eaten breakfast and began to start eating all over again. Fortunately, we remember such actions easily. Most of us succeed in giving an account of what we did during the day, or in telling someone what we did during our vacation without any trouble. The aim of this book is to show this and to explain why we remember our own actions so well.

AIMS AND ORGANISATION OF THE BOOK

In the early 1980s, Ronald Cohen (1981, 1985) in Toronto and we in Saarbrücken (Engelkamp & Krumnacker, 1980; Engelkamp & Zimmer, 1983) had begun to investigate the recollection of self-performed tasks. To do this, participants were read lists of simple, unrelated actions—such as comb your hair, open the marmalade jar, bend the wire, close the umbrella, etc.—and were requested to remember these phrases. The following comparison stood at the centre of this experiment: One group of subjects only listened to the phrases, while the other group both listened to the phrases and acted out the tasks described in each phrase. The second group recalled a great deal more of the phrases than the first (Cohen, 1981; Engelkamp & Krumnacker, 1980). I call this effect the "enactment effect". Self-performed tasks (SPTs) are recalled much better than verbal tasks (VTs) in which we have only heard the phrases. This book will enquire into the question of why self-performed tasks are recalled so well. I have two objectives here. First, I attempt to give a comprehensive overview of the research on recollection of self-performed tasks. I also attempt to show which explanations have been proposed for their good recollection and how research has been developed and modified along the lines of these proposals.

The second, broader objective is to contribute to the theory of episodic memory. It becomes clear that the investigation into the recollection of self-performed tasks has moved away from general deliberations on episodic memory, but that the further development of these deliberations has been stimulating and has brought forth new memory phenomena. Even specific laws of memory for self-performed tasks have been discussed, which are set apart from those of verbal learning (Cohen, 1981, 1985). Therefore, another goal is to contribute to the development of a general theory on episodic memory through the discussion of research on the recollection of self-performed tasks.

The structure of this book is the result of intertwining historical and systematic perspectives. Historically viewed, it started out with relatively unconnected research activities from a variety of groups. Characteristic of this phase (about 1980–85) was that all of the groups primarily concentrated on one cause for the enactment effect. They focused their research upon this and took hardly any notice of the other groups. Chapter 3 relates to this "early" research.

After the groups became aware of each other, they began to make reference to one another, particularly at conferences, but only occasionally in publications (e.g. Cohen, 1989a; Engelkamp & Zimmer, 1989; Helstrup, 1987; Zimmer & Engelkamp, 1989b). I delivered the first systematic depiction of all current findings and the various theoretical positions in my book on human memory (Engelkamp, 1990, chap. 5). In this depiction, I pointed to a series of inconsistent findings as well as controversial predictions following from the different theoretical positions. A series of experimental investigations, particularly in our own research group, was produced as a result of these inconsistent findings and controversial predictions. I report on these in Chapter 5.

One thing common to all of these research efforts was that the causes for the enactment effect were located in encoding. Only the latest research, which was begun in the 1990s, has become characterised by its calling also upon the process of retrieval in explaining the enactment effect. I give a report of this recent data in Chapter 7.

This is the historical perspective of the book's organisation. As mentioned, a systematic perspective is intertwined with this. It is no surprise that research has become more complex through the course of the years. After a good 15 years of research, we know more about the process of recollection than at the start. With this accumulation of empirical knowledge, theoretical assumptions have become more complex as well. I endeavour to convey these developments in theory by placing an attempt at integration of theory between each historically oriented chapter. These chapters on theory, Chapters 4, 6, and 8, are laid out correspondingly to introduce the theoretical differences necessary for the explanation of the previously depicted findings.

When one looks at the course of research in memory psychology over the years, it is plain that the primary focus of attention has been on the processes of encoding. The significance of the processes in retrieval were first taken note of later. The preoccupation with the interaction between encoding and retrieval has only arisen recently. This course of events in research development is also noticeable in the research of self-performed tasks, and has been reflected in the organisation of the book.

PREVIEW OF THE BOOK'S CHAPTERS

To introduce the most important dimensions of memory processes, I give a short overview in Chapter 2 on the state of theory on memory in the early 1980s. Important dimensions, besides the distinction between the encoding processes at study and retrieval processes at test, are the distinctions between item-specific and relational information and between automatic and controlled processes in encoding and retrieving. Item-specific information differentiates every single event from all others in memory. It is related to the discriminative function of memory. Relational processes create relationships between events which promote their recovery in memory. They affect the organising function of memory. Encoding and usage of both types of information, item-specific and relational, can occur with or without the use of strategies by the learner, that is either automatically or controlled.

Another common aspect of episodic recollection will be described as "encoding specificity of retrieval" (Tulving & Thomson, 1973). This refers to the fact that recollection performance is not only dependent upon the quality of encoding, but also upon the extent to which the encoded information is used in retrieval. Therefore, recollection should be at its best when the processes of retrieval agree with those of encoding.

Finally, the distinction of modality-specific memory systems was repeatedly discussed. The separation of a memory system, which specialises in verbal information, from a visual system, which specialises in nonverbal visual information, received particular attention (Paivio, 1971, 1986). As a rule it was claimed that the visual memory system is more efficient than the verbal system. Other sensory systems, in particular motor systems, received hardly any notice.

Once again, it should be noted that these three dimensions—item-specific/relational, automatic/controlled, and various coding systems—were introduced and studied independently of each other.

These three dimensions also represent the central dimensions for the explanation of memory of self-performed tasks. On its own, however, that would not be exciting. It would simply confirm what has chiefly been achieved through verbal memory research. What is exciting and important for theorising on episodic recollection of self-performed tasks is, first of all, that the quality of recollection of self-performed tasks evidently does not rely upon strategic encoding. Second, relational encoding appears to be less crucial for the good recollection of self-performed tasks than for verbal tasks. Third, motor processes, which up to that point had been entirely omitted as a determinant in recollection, appear to be significant for the recollection of self-performed tasks.

These aspects constitute the subject of Chapter 3. In this chapter investigations will be reported that corroborate these properties of the recollection of self-performed tasks. The encoding process during learning stood at the centre of each hypothesis on the recollection of self-performed tasks. Cohen (1981, 1983) made observations that led him to postulate that the encoding of self-performed tasks occurs free from strategy. Bäckman and Nilsson (e.g. 1985) traced the enactment effect back to multimodal encoding processes. According to these authors, verbal as well as nonverbal multimodal encoding processes have a role in actions initiated by verbal commands. This richness of encoding is the reason for the good recollection of self-performed tasks. In addition, they assume that verbal processes are controlled and that nonverbal processes are automatic. Engelkamp and Zimmer (1985) ascribe the high quality of recollection of enacted actions to the specific motor components of their encoding. In particular, they contrast the sensory and motor encoding processes. Finally, what was most widespread, although admittedly not until the latter half of the 1980s, was the idea that good recollection of self-performed actions could be traced back to particularly good item-specific encoding processes (Bäckman & Nilsson, 1985; Cohen, 1981; Engelkamp, 1988; Engelkamp & Zimmer, 1985; Helstrup, 1987; Knopf & Neidhardt, 1989; Saltz, 1988).

Chapter 4 attempts to integrate all of these hypotheses into the framework of one theory, the multimodal memory theory, and to explain the various findings within this framework. The multimodal memory theory not only integrates the findings involved, it also shows that a series of hypotheses and findings are contradictory and it leads to a series of new predictions.

It is the object of Chapter 5 to clarify these inconsistencies and theoretical controversies as well as to test a series of hypotheses that can be derived from the multimodal memory theory. These points are addressed in brief here.

One assumption of the multimodal memory theory, which derives from other theoretical assumptions, concerns the role of sensory encoding processes in the enactment effect. According to the assumptions of Bäckman and Nilsson (1985), sensory and motor aspects should contribute equally to the enactment effect. In contrast, according to the multimodal theory, the elements of motor encoding are critical (Engelkamp & Zimmer, 1985). One aspect in which these different assumptions become relevant is the use of actual objects. According to Bäckman and Nilsson (1985), the advantage of performance through the use of concrete objects (in contrast to imagined objects) should be especially large (e.g. through the encoding of form, texture, colour, etc. of the object used). According to the multimodal memory theory, the use of actual objects should not be critical for the advantage of performance, that is, for the size of the enactment effect.

One other controversial aspect concerns the perception of tasks carried out by another person. Interestingly, Cohen was unable to establish any difference in retention between self-performed and experimenter-performed tasks (EPTs) (e.g. Cohen, 1989a). Cohen therefore presumes that the encoding processes differentiate little between viewed and performed tasks. This stands in opposition to the assumptions of Bäckman and Nilsson as well as of Engelkamp and Zimmer, according to which there are no motor encoding processes involved in EPTs. In addition, Engelkamp and Zimmer (e.g. Engelkamp, 1990, chap. 5) consistently observed better retention after enactment than after observation of actions.

Similar inconsistencies lie in the findings about whether simply planning to perform an action improves retention in comparison to listening to descriptions of actions and, if that is the case, whether carrying out the action improves retention further (Brooks & Gardiner, 1994; Koriat, Ben-Zur, & Nussbaum, 1990; Zimmer & Engelkamp, 1984). The latter should be the case according to the multimodal memory theory (Engelkamp, 1990, Chap. 5).

Finally, according to Engelkamp and Zimmer (1985) and the multimodal memory theory, motor similarities between the actions to be memorised and the distractor actions should negatively affect recognition after enactment. The findings here are contradictory as well. Cohen (1989b) explicitly embraces the idea that the type of movement is not critical for the retention of self-performed tasks.

A further controversy refers to relational encoding processes. According to the multimodal theory, the use of pre-experimental semantic knowledge in relational encoding processes should not differ between verbal learning and learning by enactment. The acquisition of new associations between actions and between actions and the places where these actions happen to take place should actually be more difficult with enactment. The multimodal theory differs in this respect from the positions of Bäckman and Nilsson (1985), as well as those of Helstrup (1989b). Findings with regard to these positions are inconsistent as well.

One final controversy concerns the question of whether or not self-performed tasks are encoded automatically (Cohen, 1981, 1983), or are both automatic *and* controlled (Bäckman & Nilsson, 1985). Inconsistent findings also accompany this controversy.

The goal of Chapter 5 is to sort out these controversies and to enquire into the causes for the inconsistent findings. This effort promotes a series of new findings, which were not predicted by any theory. These findings are compiled in Chapter 6 and related to the multimodal memory theory.

Chapter 7 concerns itself with the latest findings, which relate to encoding through enactment on the one side and retrieval processes in testing on the other. These findings, too, were partially unforeseen. The new findings on encoding pertain to the influence of the individual structure of action phrases. Until recently, all action phrases were viewed as functionally equivalent with regard to the enactment effect. This position was most recently revised by Kormi-Nouri (1995). Another new observation is that self-performing a task as a simulation of an observed action leads to different retention than carrying it out following a verbal command (Zimmer & Engelkamp, 1996). These findings also demand further revision of the theoretical conjectures.

One particularly meaningful revision of the theoretical surmises results from new findings relating to retrieval processes. These findings show that SPTs lead to a different serial position curve in free recall than VTs and that—related to this—the pattern of findings following levels of processing instructions after SPTs also differ from those after VTs. They also show that recognition after enactment shows a few idiosyncrasies. All of these findings force us to search for the causes of the enactment effect not only in encoding, but also in retrieval, and particularly in the interaction between encoding and retrieval processes. With this it becomes clear that the principle of encoding specificity is all too simple. This complicating of encoding specificity goes back to a substantial degree to the fact that the processes underlying the various test conditions were too simply conceptualised. Among other things, this becomes noticeable in findings on the serial position curve in free recall (Zimmer, Helstrup, Engelkamp, & Saathoff, 1997), as well as in the findings on recognition (Zimmer & Engelkamp, in press). Chapter 8 serves to integrate these new findings on encoding and retrieval with the multimodal memory theory.

This step-by-step expansion of the finding's status and the corresponding gradual differentiation of the theoretical assumptions do not only reflect the actual course of research in this area, but should also (at least that is my hope) make it easier to understand these assumptions, which in the meantime have become quite complicated.

Although similar differentiations can be observed in memory theory in general, the necessity of this differentiation is clearer in the investigation of self-performed tasks than in the other areas of memory research. The role of motor behaviour as an encoding factor becomes directly obvious only with SPTs. Chapter 9 serves to compile once again the implications of the investigation of self-performed tasks for the theory on memory in general.

In Chapter 10, the perspective is widened. Where memory for self-performed actions is relevant in everyday life will be discussed. The focus here is on the impact of the exploration of the good memory of SPTs as presented in this book for explaining failures to remember one's own action in everyday life. In this final chapter, the relationship between SPT research and research of prospective memory will also be discussed.

CHAPTER TWO

Explanations for episodic memory

In this chapter, I concern myself primarily with the development of research into episodic memory up to approximately 1980. An important change in the explanations for episodic performance was the switch from the multi-store model of memory (Atkinson & Shiffrin, 1968; Shiffrin & Atkinson, 1969) to the process-oriented approach of levels of processing (Craik & Lockhart, 1972). Other alternatives to the multi-store model of memory were the code theories of memory. The dual code theory of Paivio (1969, 1971) became especially well-known. Both hypotheses—process theory and code theory—were differentiated and developed during the course of the 1970s. These developments and differentiations will be traced in this chapter, since they represent the background for the explanation of the enactment effect (cf. Engelkamp, 1994, 1995a). I want to show that, for the most part, three lines of development are relevant for the explanation of episodic recollection within the context in question. Two of these developments focus on the process approach, the other on the code approach. All developments emerged relatively independent of each other; there was no integration of the various approaches.

ITEM-SPECIFIC VERSUS RELATIONAL PROCESSES

According to the influential explanation for episodic retention by Craik and Lockhart (1972), retention is the inevitable result of the processes which take place during encoding. To influence these processes is to influence retention.

9

What is critical for retention is not the intention to retain something, but rather the stimulation of the right encoding processes. Encoding processes progress along three levels: from a structural level, over a phonemic one, to a semantic level. The further the encoding process advances, that is, the deeper the level reached, the better the retention. In experimental studies, orienting tasks can determine how far the encoding process advances.

Two aspects of this proposal deserve particular attention. First, what is retained depends upon which encoding processes take place. Second, that the encoding processes treated by Craik and Lockhart concern item-specific information, or information that relates to single items and makes these items distinct from others.

Whereas Craik and Lockhart (1972) concentrated on item-specific information as the main determiner for episodic recollection, Mandler (1967; 1968) considered relational information as decisive for retention. For him, the organisation processes, which connect the items of a list of items among each other, form the nucleus of encoding. Mandler stimulated these processes by directing his subjects to sort items according to given criteria into a predetermined number of categories. Other authors manipulated the structure of the lists to vary relational encoding (e.g. Kintsch, 1968). The type of memory test was not discussed as being of any great theoretical importance within this approach either. In general, retention was tested as free recall. In addition, organisational scores reflecting the degree of relational encoding were developed on the basis of the items recollected in free recall (e.g. Roenker, Thompson, & Brown,1971).

Even when neither the levels of processing approach nor the organisation-oriented approach have dealt theoretically with the processes at test, the assumption is plausible that a "deeper" processing improves the distinctiveness of the items, whereas a better connection among the items should make their generation at test easier. The processes during testing were the explicit theme of the so-called "generation-recognition" models. Two processes become differentiated during the test: the generation of information in search processes, and the decision of whether or not the information thus generated belongs to the learning episode (Bahrick, 1970; Kintsch, 1970). The differentiation of these two components of processing in retrieval also allows us to explain the difference between free recall and recognition memory. In free recall, memory traces are generated, and it is then decided whether or not these traces belong to the episode. In recognition memory, the generation of potential memory traces is unnecessary because the items are presented directly by the experimenter for an episodic decision. Similar differentiations were suggested by Raaijmakers and Shiffrin (1981) and by Gillund and Shiffrin (1984). Although the terms "item-specific" and "relational" information are not used in the context of "generation-recognition" models, it is obvious that the generation process refers to relational information, and the decision process to item-specific information.

A further differentiation is introduced through the principle of encoding specificity (Tulving & Thomson, 1973). In this proposal retention is viewed as the common result of encoding and retrieval processes. For example, the more similar the situation is in retrieval to that of encoding, the more successful the search for the information to be recollected should be. The concept here of "situation" refers to the common context information at study and at test. It was the idea of Tulving and Thomson (1973) that context words, which were presented during learning together with the items to be memorised, could be helpful later at test as retrieval cues. This benefit should be specific to the item involved and the item context should be effective because of its episodic connection with the item and not because of pre-experimental item-context associations. The principle of encoding specificity soon became applied to the context of whole learning lists as well, for example to the physical location where learning and recalling of the list took place (e.g. Godden & Baddeley, 1975).

The principle of encoding specificity, to the extent to which it has been presented so far, has two related weaknesses. It is based primarily on the concept of context, and this is unclear (cf. Clark & Carlson, 1981). Furthermore, it is unable to explain why list contexts work to help with recall, but not with recognition (Eich, 1980; Godden & Baddeley, 1980; Smith, Glenberg, & Bjork, 1979). Both of these problems are solved when the principle of encoding specificity is related to the differentiation between item-specific and relational information and then connected to the "generation-recognition" theory. Since free recall is based on relational *and* item-specific information, it should profit from both types of information encoding in episodic learning. In comparison, recognition memory should benefit chiefly from item-specific encoding, since it is based significantly on this. To my knowledge, these links were first examined experimentally by Einstein and Hunt (1980) and by Hunt and Einstein (1981), though they did not refer to the principle of encoding specificity by Tulving and Thomson (1973). Hunt and Einstein (1981) showed that item-specific encoding during learning influenced recognition. However, it had little influence upon organisational scores, which reflect the relational information in recall. In opposition to this, the degree of organisation in recall varied with the relational encoding during learning, while recognition remained uninfluenced by relational encoding. In turn, retention performance in free recall depended on item-specific *and* relational encoding during learning.

Up to this point, a relatively coherent picture is shown. Item-specific and relational information are encoded during the learning of lists. Depending upon the type of test, they can also be used in the test phase.

AUTOMATIC VERSUS CONTROLLED PROCESSES

Around 1980, independent of the discrimination between item-specific and relational information, attention was drawn to the distinction between automatic and controlled processes. At first, these two concepts were not defined exactly, they were used quite heterogenously and they were introduced within the context of attention research (e.g. Wessels, 1984, chap. 3). Most supported the idea that controlled processes are conscious, are accompanied by the experience of effort, and are available only to a limited extent. Furthermore, they can be interfered with by other controlled processes. Automatic processes, on the other hand, occur precisely without these conscious controls. Therefore, they are not experienced as effortful and any given number of these processes can occur simultaneously. Finally, they are not interfered with by controlled processes. The so-called dual task paradigm is used as proof for controlled processes. Two tasks, which are carried out simultaneously and which both place demand upon controlled processes, should disrupt each other reciprocally. Tasks that are based upon automatic processes should not be disrupted by secondary tasks (for a critical discussion see Engelkamp, 1990, chap. 2.4; Neumann, 1992; Smyth, Morris, Levy, & Ellis, 1987, chap. 5).

This disruption between two tasks, also described as central interference, should however be differentiated from structural interference. Structural interference is also brought about through double tasks, but its ties to research on attention are looser. It refers to the assumption that two tasks, which use the same part systems, interfere reciprocally with each other by overwriting. With regard to memory performance, this means that the performance of one task is adversely affected when a second task uses the same structure (Engelkamp, 1990, chap. 4.5).

Altogether, the distinction between automatic and controlled processes was hardly paid any attention in memory psychology for a long time. With regard to encoding processes, Hasher and Zacks (1979) directed attention to the differentiation of automatic and controlled processes. They assumed that there are a number of specific aspects of stimuli (such as location or frequency of occurrence), which are encoded automatically with the stimulus. Specific to their suggestion was the assumption that these automatic encoding processes were inborn and could be neither changed nor influenced. According to Hasher and Zacks, the retention of these stimulus aspects should therefore be independent from the age of the subjects, of practice, of the intention of learning, and so on. It soon became obvious that these claims go too far and cannot be confirmed empirically (e.g. McDaniel, Einstein, & Lollis, 1988; Naveh-Benjamin, 1987).

All in all, the distinction between automatic and controlled processes in learning were discussed and investigated astonishingly little up into the

1980s. However, it was generally assumed that retention was improved through elaborate encoding, for example through active thinking of definitions (e.g. Craik & Lockhart, 1972), or through actively forming associations (e.g. Mandler, 1967). These processes were referred to as controlled encoding. In opposition, when encoding did not ensue actively, one spoke of automatic encoding processes. Automatic encoding processes should be more difficult to influence than controlled encoding processes, precisely because they are automatic. The fundamental value of this dichotomy lies in the assumption that encoding processes can be influenced to different degrees.

Various suggestions for the differentiation of automatic and controlled processes were also made for the test situation, specifically in consideration of recognition memory. Mandler (Graf & Mandler, 1984; Mandler, 1980; Mandler, Goodman, & Wilkes-Gibbs, 1982) suggested that the combination of two different processes led to recognition memory performance because of the additive effects of certain factors, such as the frequency of occurrence of words and the depth of their processing (Mandler et al., 1982). According to Mandler, occurrence frequency led to automatic recognition and pro-cessing depth to controlled recognition. Admittedly, instead of "automatic" and "controlled", Mandler speaks of familiarity-based, or integration-based, and elaboration-based recognition. Recognition is based on famil-iarity when the automatic activation of an integrated, pre-experimental representation in memory is used to make an old–new decision. In contrast, recognition is elaboration based when the relationships established during the learning episode between the items are used for deciding upon recog-nition. In this case, the person searches more or less actively (controlled) for the information that was encoded during the learning episode.

Similar suggestions were made by Jacoby (1983; Jacoby & Dallas, 1981). Also, according to him, automatic processes as well as controlled processes can make the items recognisable as "old".

One problem shared by Mandler's (1980) and Jacoby's (1983) suggestions is the unsatisfactory operationalising of the concepts "automatic" and "controlled". It is difficult to indicate how one can establish whether automatic or controlled recognition takes place. Suggestions for this were first made a few years later (e.g. Gardiner, 1988; Jacoby, 1991).

VARIOUS CODES

Consideration of modality-specific encoding has played practically no role in the process aspects discussed so far. One exception to this is the brief mention of structural interference and the levels of processing approach which distinguishes between non-semantic and semantic encoding processes, even though this approach was not brought into connection with code theories. Even so, the distinction between nonsemantic and semantic information is central to nearly every code theory (e.g. Nelson, 1979; Wippich, 1981). The influential dual code theory of Paivio (1971) is one exception to this.

Paivio suggested quite early (1969, 1971) differentiating between a verbal code system for the encoding of linguistic stimuli, and a nonverbal code system for the encoding of nonverbal stimuli. By nonverbal stimuli here, I will restrict myself to picture stimuli. The picture superiority effect (Madigan, 1983), for example, is explained by this differentiation. More object names are retained when the objects are presented during learning than when merely the words are given.

Here I would like to briefly discuss two problematic aspects of the dual code theory. First, Paivio explicitly abstains from differentiating between semantic and nonsemantic information. He speaks of verbal-semantic and imaginal-semantic. This abstention from an explicit separation of non-semantic and semantic information is problematic because it prevents the investigation of the influence of both types of information on retention independently of each other. Second, Paivio does not take into consideration that stimulus modalities differentiate themselves functionally from (both verbal and nonverbal) code modalities. Although Paivio noted that the symbolic systems (verbal/nonverbal) are different from the sensory-motor systems (visual/auditory/haptic/gustatory/olfactory), he does not make this differentiation explicit with regard to the functional assumptions of his theory (cf. Paivio, 1986, p. 67). Only verbal and nonverbal codes are mentioned in the explanation of retention differences.

A differentiation between semantic and nonsemantic codes can, however, be found in every other code theory (e.g. Nelson, 1979; Snodgrass, 1984; Wippich, 1981). These theories explicitly assume that objects, or events, and their verbal descriptions possess common semantic representations for their meanings. The meaning of two stimuli, for example a picture of an apple and the word "apple", is the same, despite the differences in modality. Because of this, a presemantic or nonsemantic code is postulated along with a semantic code. I also speak of a conceptual code instead of a semantic code. Usually, the presemantic codes are characterised as acoustic and visual. With this, it is important to differentiate between linguistic and nonlinguistic stimuli.

It is often assumed that words presented visually are recoded phonemically (e.g. Garnham, 1985). To a certain extent, Craik and Lockhart (1972) assume phonemic recoding as well. They assume that with a visual presentation of words, phonemic processing follows structural processing.

Proof of the necessity for the distinction between phonemic, visual-nonverbal, and semantic information can be found, for instance, in the studies of Nelson and his colleagues (Nelson, 1979). Nelson was able to show that semantic similarity affected equally the retention of pictures and their descriptions. However, visual similarities, for example similarities in shape, only affected the retention of pictures, and only the retention of their verbal descriptions was affected by phonemic similarities. Nelson's findings not only prove that phonemic, visual-nonverbal, and semantic information are encoded separately, they also prove that the assumption of dual encoding of pictures and concrete words is not tenable. If this were the case, phonemic similarities would have to affect the retention of pictures, whereas visual similarities, correlating to similarities in shape, would have to affect the retention of words.

The idea of modality-specific code systems can be found in a different context in Baddeley and Hitch as well (1974; see also Baddeley, 1986). In his model of working memory, Baddeley postulates two peripheral-memory systems in addition to an attention-based central system; he does not refer to a semantic system. He calls these systems phonological loop and "visual-spatial sketch pad". Later, Logie (1991) discusses a visual-spatial working memory. The phonological loop specialises in processing verbal stimuli. It consists of a phonological store and an articulatory rehearsal mechanism. The latter serves to hinder the fast decay of phonological information. To a certain degree, this cache supports the transfer of information to the semantic system. The visual-spatial working memory was structured later, analogous to the verbal-acoustic working memory (Logie, e.g. 1991). Both working memory systems are supported by experimental findings (Baddeley, 1986; Logie, 1995).

To sum up: Modality-specific aspects of stimuli influence memory performance and this influence is independent of their semantic meaning. Therefore, it is useful to take modality-specific aspects into account in the theory of episodic memory.

SUMMARY

At the beginning of the 1980s, when the experimental examination of retention of self-performed tasks began, the following aspects were viewed as important factors in episodic memory.

1. *Item-specific and relational information.* Whether the learning episode was more likely to be encoded item-specifically than relationally or the other way round, and to what extent this information was encoded, was considered to be critical. Another important factor was to what extent the information was used at testing.
2. *Automatic and controlled processes.* The possibility of variable encoding was seen as dependent upon whether the encoding was achieved automatically or controlled. Automatic encoding processes

should tend to be invariant and not very easily influenced. Controlled encoding processes, on the other hand, tend to be flexible and easy to influence. With regard to retention, at least to recognition memory, it was also assumed that performance could be either automatic or controlled.

3. *Code systems.* In code theories, retention was not only viewed as dependent upon the meaning of the stimuli, but also upon their physical characteristics. Therefore modality-specific code systems were assumed for the encoding of these characteristics or stimulus modalities.

Each of the different research traditions focused on one of these aspects and practically no attempts at integration took place. It is therefore not surprising that the studies on recollection of self-performed tasks around 1980 were also concentrated on these aspects and that integration efforts were absent here as well.

CHAPTER THREE

Early findings and explanations for the retention of self-performed tasks

With the general principles for the explanation of episodic memory represented in Chapter 2 as a backdrop, different explanations soon developed for the memory advantage of self-performed tasks (SPTs) in comparison to verbal tasks (VTs). It will become clear that these explanations pick up on these general principles. Their findings, which support these principles, will be represented in this chapter. First, I would like to examine the research paradigm and its variations and bring the enactment effect into recollection.

In the early phase, the research paradigm contained the following consistent characteristics. Identical lists of action phrases were listened to in VTs and additionally acted out in SPTs. The two encoding conditions were varied between subjects. In both tasks, an intentional learning situation was at hand. The rate of presentation was approximately 5 seconds per item. Usually, the memory of action phrases was measured through free recall, and only seldom through a recognition test (e.g. Engelkamp & Krumnacker, 1980; Schaaf, 1988). Particularly variable factors were the length of the lists (which varied between 12 and 48 items) and the type of the action phrases that the lists contained. These could be mixed (with body-related items such as "nod with your head", and with object-related items such as "smoke a pipe"), or pure (only object-related items). The objects in the SPT condition were either given as actual objects, or they were "imaginary", that is, the subjects acted as if they used the object. In this case I also speak of symbolic performance. The action phrases were presented either in the imperative ("bend the wire"), or in the infinitive ("to bend the wire"). Helstrup and

Molander (1996) were recently able to show that this variation does not influence the enactment effect.

The superiority of enactment was equally observed under different conditions (such as short vs. long lists, pure vs. mixed lists, real vs. imaginary objects) (e.g. Bäckman, 1985; Cohen, 1981; Engelkamp & Krumnacker, 1980; see Engelkamp, 1990, chap. 5 for an overview). That is, the enactment effect is an extremely robust effect.

During the early research phase, this basic effect was then examined with dependence on such variables focused upon in each explanation. In addition, it was more generally studied whether learning through enactment was influenced by the same variables as verbal learning.

ENACTMENT AS STRATEGY-FREE ENCODING

Cohen (1981, 1983, 1985) investigated whether retention of self-performed tasks was influenced by the same variables as verbal learning. He was interested in whether certain central phenomena of verbal learning could also be observed in SPT learning. In this, he even refers to "memory laws" for verbal learning. The first two phenomena studied by him were the serial position curve in free recall and the effect of depth of processing.

The serial position effect is based upon the fact that the first and last items represented in a list are recalled better than those positioned in the middle. The primacy effect goes back to the idea that the items first represented are rehearsed more often and are therefore able to be recalled better than those offered later (their rehearsal competes with that of the items already presented and this increases with each additional item). The recency effect, among others, is explained by the idea that it goes back to the acoustic short-term memory. The last items represented are still found in this memory (Glanzer & Schwartz, 1971). Rundus (1971) demonstrated the connection between rehearsal and recall of items by instructing his subjects to rehearse aloud. In that way he could identify how often each item was rehearsed. The connection between the rehearsal frequency and the retention of the items in the first half of the list was impressive. As expected, it disappeared by the last part of the list. I embellish upon other explanations for the serial position curve in Chapter 7.

The effect of levels of processing goes back to Craik and Lockhart (1972). It consists of the idea that items that are "deeply", that is semantically processed are recalled better than "shallow", that is nonsemantically processed items. This effect was observed repeatedly for verbal learning (e.g. Craik & Tulving, 1975; Hyde & Jenkins, 1969).

Both effects were explained by the idea that better encoding results in more information being retained and that better encoding is obtained by rehearsal and elaboration of the items to be learned. This elaboration is at the same time seen as controlled encoding. This assumption is supported in that retention is dependent on the age and intelligence of the learner. The more intelligent someone is, the better their ability in controlled encoding, and the better their retention. This is similarly true for age. Ability in active encoding first increases with age (from childhood to early adulthood) and then decreases again with advancing years (Craik & Jennings, 1992).

Cohen (1981) compared the serial position curve under a listening condition and an enactment condition with lists containing 15 items. He found that, in contrast to listening, no primacy effect was observed in the enactment condition. This is illustrated in Fig. 3.1. This effect has been reproduced repeatedly (e.g. Bäckman & Nilsson, 1984, 1985; Cohen, 1983; Cohen & Bean, 1983; Cohen & Stewart, 1982; Knopf & Neidhardt, 1989).

The other effect investigated by Cohen (1981) for recall of action phrases after VTs and SPTs is the effect of depth of processing. On the one hand, subjects had to judge actions according to how much noise they cause or by the degree to which they involve the entire body ("shallow" encoding). On the other hand, the actions had to be judged according to how often the subjects performed the task and when the last time was that they had done this ("deep" encoding according to Cohen). While the usual effect of depth of processing was observed following VTs (0.42 vs. 0.60), no such effect could be observed following SPTs (0.49 vs. 0.50).

Because Cohen (1981) was neither able to observe a primacy effect, nor an effect of levels of processing, he descriptively ascertained that particular variables, such as rehearsal and depth of processing, have little relevance for

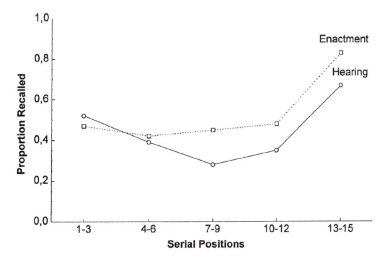

FIG. 3.1.   Serial position curve in free recall after hearing and enactment (adapted from Cohen, 1981, Exp. 1).

learning through enactment, in spite of being central in verbal learning. Just two years later, however, he went distinctly further with his conclusions. Cohen (1983) then regarded the nonappearance of the primacy and depth of processing effects after enactment as indicating that the encoding processes in enactment are nonstrategic, that is automatic.

In further experiments, Cohen aimed at finding additional support for the assumption that enactment can be equated with automatic encoding. Cohen (1983) manipulated controlled processing of the items by asking his subjects to pay more attention to some items than to others. This procedure had also proven effective in verbal learning (Bjork, 1972; Harley, 1965). The importance of items had little influence on retention after enactment. Similarly, Cohen (1983) observed that the subjects under enactment conditions were hardly able to predict which actions they would be able to retain better or worse. However, under listening conditions they were able to predict their retention performance for particular items. Cohen views these findings as further support for his assumption that verbal learning tends to be strategy-dependent, while learning through enactment is automatic, that is strategy-free. Therefore, the employment of strategic encoding processes can improve verbal learning but not learning through enactment.

The hypothesis of automatic encoding through enactment was supported subsequently by further findings. Helstrup (1987) and Zimmer (1984) manipulated the extent of elaboration by encoding by having the subjects perform a varying number of preparatory tasks for another task which was to be learned. For example, if the item "to light a match" was to be learned, this task could be performed directly (little elaboration). It could also be performed with much more elaboration, for example a matchbox is opened, a match is taken out, the box is closed, and then the match is struck and lit. Neither author was able to observe a difference in retention performance under the instruction to carry out the goal task directly and under the instruction to also perform the preparatory tasks.

Despite all difficulties connected with the operationalising depth of processing, it can be maintained that no elaboration effect through enactment was observed in any of these studies.

In this context it is also important that no generation effect appears after enactment. The opposite is true after listening. The generation effect is viewed as an effect of conceptual elaboration (see Gardiner, Gregg, & Hampton, 1988; or Engelkamp, 1990, chap. 6.4.3). This effect was demonstrated repeatedly after verbal learning. For the most part in the generation experiments, a reading condition as a control condition for words is compared with a generation condition. In the generation condition the subjects must form the words themselves (e.g. solving anagrams or completing word fragments). In the generation condition, Nilsson and Cohen (1988), like

Lichty, Bressie, and Krell (1988), were unable to observe a generation effect after SPTs. Nilsson and Cohen (1988) presented their subjects with an object for which they should generate, name, and execute a task. In the control condition, the subjects were told the task for the object, which they then performed. Analogous to this, the subjects for the listening condition had to generate action phrases for object words, or they simply listened to the phrases (control). While no generation effect appeared after enactment, one was found, as expected, after listening.

Another variable related to active encoding processes is encoding time. The slower the presentation rate, the more time available for processing, the more active encoding processes should be brought into action, and the better retention should be. This holds true in verbal learning (e.g. Glanzer & Cunitz, 1966; Murdock, 1960). Cohen (1985) could show that the presentation time was not critical for retention after SPTs (but cf. Cohen & Bryant, 1991).

Kausler and his colleagues reported a comparable finding (Kausler, 1982; Kausler, Litchy, & Davis, 1985; Kausler, Litchy, & Freund, 1985; Kausler, Litchy, Hakami, & Freund, 1986). They used a slightly different paradigm. They had their subjects perform simple activities. Some of these were motor activities (e.g. cutting out shapes) and some were mental activities (e.g. completing words). At the end, the subjects should recall the activities (not the individual actions). It was found that the duration for which the activities were carried out (between 45 and 180 seconds) did not influence retention performance.

These different findings support the assumption that enactment encoding is automatic and that elaboration does not play a role. If this is true, also effects of intelligence and age on learning self-performed tasks should be minimal. This was proved in various experiments. For example, Cohen and Stewart (1982) observed age-dependent recall of action phrases in children between 9 and 13 years following verbal learning, but not after enactment. Similarly, Cohen and Bean (1983) found a difference in recall of word lists between normal children and slightly mentally retarded children. However, such a difference was not found for the recall of action phrases after enactment.

All of these findings supported Cohen's (1983, 1985) assumption that encoding through enactment is strategy-free. An obvious problem, which is not solved in Cohen's hypothesis of strategy-free encoding, is the explanation for the enactment effect itself. Automatic encoding through enactment still does not explain why this encoding is so good. On the contrary, according to the concept of strategic encoding it is to be expected that strategic encoding processes are more efficient than automatic. As a solution to this problem, Bäckman and Nilsson contribute their hypothesis of rich, multimodal encoding through enactment.

ENACTMENT OF ACTIONS AS RICH, MULTIMODAL ENCODING

Bäckman and Nilsson (Bäckman & Nilsson, 1984, 1985; Bäckman, Nilsson, & Chalom, 1986) specified the considerations on strategy-free encoding through enactment as proposed by Cohen (1983, 1985).

Bäckman (1985; Bäckman & Nilsson, 1984, 1985) also observed an age effect with VTs, but no such effect with SPTs. They compared retention of older adults with young adults. In addition to this, Bäckman and Nilsson (1984) made the following observation: Some of the phrases contained an object (e.g. "lift up the pen"), and some did not (e.g. "nod your head"). It appeared that in the enactment condition their subjects had organised the phrases according to this aspect during recall. In view of this, they analysed the data and found that the phrases were clustered according to whether there had been an object or not. After enactment the ARC score (0.50) was greater than after listening (0.20) (cf. also Bäckman & Nilsson, 1985). The ARC score stands for Adjusted Ratio of Clustering and goes back to Roenker et al. (1971). It was constructed to determine the extent to which subjects organised their free recall along category structures of a list (here: items with and without an external object). The items were presented in a random order. Therefore the organising of the items in free recall into categories can be seen as an indication that the subjects had encoded the categorical structure. The higher the ARC score, the better the categorical structure of the lists are encoded.

Going from this observation, Bäckman et al. (1986) constructed a list of 25 phrases, which were organised according to 5 categories (actions with clothes items, actions with toys, actions with kitchen appliances, actions with pencil and paper, e.g. "write down a number", and body-related actions). These lists were presented for learning under both listening and enactment conditions, as well as with or without interference. The interference task consisted of alternately subtracting 3 and 6 from 600 during learning. An enactment effect was observed. More was retained by enactment than by listening. The subtraction task was disruptive and it had a stronger effect under the listening condition. The performances in recall are summarised in Table 3.1.

TABLE 3.1
Relative performance in free recall under listening and enactment conditions as well as with and without an interference task (Bäckman, Nilsson, & Chalom, 1986)

	Enactment	Listening
Without interference	0.78	0.45
With interference	0.61	0.16

Apart from recall, clustering was analysed. More clustering occured after enactment than after listening. The interaction between encoding conditions and interference tasks was not significant, although all ARC scores, with the exception of the ARC score after listening with interference (–0.10) were greater than 0.30 and positive (Table 3.2).

In a second experiment, Bäckman et al. (1986) compared retention for the organised list with the retention of an unorganised list of different phrases. There was better retention after SPTs than after VTs and a greater decrease in retention from the organised list to the unorganised list after SPTs than after VTs. Since the unorganized list contained unrelated items, no ARC scores were calculated for this experiment.

Bäckman et al. conclude from these findings that enacted phrases are retained better because, first, the actions carried out from the phrases represent multimodal experiences including features such as colour, texture, shape, and sound, which are encoded automatically. These features are absent under the listening condition. Here, only verbal features are encoded. The encoding from enactment is always richer, that is in organised as well as unorganised lists. Second, the verbal features are encoded under the enactment condition as well. This verbal information is not encoded automatically, but rather strategically. It also makes available information that forms the organisation of the list. This information should be easier to use after enactment, that is under the influence of rich multimodal encoding, than after listening. It increases the enactment effect. This means that the subjects in enactment profit in two respects from organised lists. They profit once from the automatic, nonverbal, multimodal, rich encoding of the action. Then they benefit again from the strategic encoding of the verbal features which make the information about the list's structure more accessible than is the case after listening.

The central extension and differentiation of this position in comparison to that of Cohen (e.g. 1985) therefore is threefold: (1) a double encoding of verbal *and* non-verbal information is assumed in enactment; (2) strategic encoding is also allowed in enactment, but just for the verbal information; (3) the multimodal character and richness of nonverbal encoding are emphasised. The assumption of multimodal, rich encoding

TABLE 3.2

Mean ARC scores under listening and enactment conditions as well as with and without an interference task (Bäckman, Nilsson, & Chalom, 1986)

	Enactment	*Listening*
Without interference	0.48	0.33
With interference	0.46	–0.10

delivers the central argument for better retention after enactment than after listening.

The encoding processes suggested by Bäckman and Nilsson (1984) for SPTs also lead to a slightly different explanation for the absence of an age effect than in Cohen's (1983, 1985) interpretation. Controlled processes also play a role in learning through enactment and exert influence upon the organisation processes. Therefore, the lack of an age effect in enactment is not just based on automatic encoding processes. Bäckman and Nilsson (1984) consequently introduce the hypothesis of spontaneous recoding. They explain the retention advantage under verbal conditions for young adults in comparison to older adults with the idea that the younger subjects spontaneously grab at organisational strategies, while the older subjects do not. For this, the older subjects need the inducement from rich multimodal stimuli. These make it possible for them to recode and compensate for their recoding deficit. In the words of Bäckman and Nilsson (1984, p. 65): "the memory task presented in a multimodal and contextually rich encoding environment gives rise to optimal organisational strategies among older adults, who thereby are capable of performing at the same level as the younger adults as well as organising the to-be-remembered materials as efficiently; the cognitive keyword is compensation."

With their concept of multimodal, rich encoding, Bäckman and Nilsson have differentiated the explanation of the effects for retention performance after enactment fundamentally. In particular, with the assumption of multimodal, rich encoding through enactment, they have offered a plausible explanation for why encoding from enactment is so good. Cohen (e.g. 1985) had admittedly made it clear that encoding is strategy-free during enactment. However, the question of why retention should be so good following strategy-free encoding remained unanswered by him. Although Bäckman and Nilsson make the observation plausible that counting backwards is disruptive under listening and enactment through their assumption that both automatic and controlled processes take part in SPT learning, the difference between automatic and controlled processes remains vague. These authors follow the general assumption that automatic processes allow the simultaneous deployment of controlled processes without being interfered with themselves. They also follow the assumption that controlled, that is attention-demanding, processes can be disrupted by other controlled processes, because they both compete for attention (Navon & Gopher, 1979; Schneider & Shiffrin, 1977; cf. also Chapter 2). Although these assumptions make it plausible that disruptive effects showed up following enactment and listening, it was not clear enough why the extent of interference from counting backwards should be greater after listening than after enactment. From the assumption that the encoding of nonverbal features ought to occur automatically in enactment, it does not necessarily follow that controlled encoding processes, which refer to verbal information, decline in comparison to listening. How the nonverbal encoding processes influence the verbal ones, with regard to their attention-demanding characteristics, is not clear. Nor is it taken into consideration that greater interference following listening than enactment could also be caused by more structural interference following listening (cf. Chapter 2). Finally, it remains unanswered how the different null-effects after enactment (with the exception of the age effect) are to be explained. These null-effects had led Cohen (e.g. 1985) to the assumption of strategy-free encoding in enactment.

ENACTMENT AS MOTOR ENCODING

Engelkamp and Zimmer (e.g. 1985) have taken the idea of modality-specific systems and encoding processes as their take-off point for investigating and explaining the enactment effect. They did not bring up the idea of automatic and strategic processes.

Like Bäckman and Nilsson (1984, 1985; Bäckman et al., 1986), they distinguish between verbal and nonverbal encoding processes. Just as Bäckman and Nilsson did, they start from the idea of multimodal encoding for nonverbal processes. In contrast to Bäckman and Nilsson (1985), Engelkamp and Zimmer concentrate on motor encoding processes and ascribe the enactment effect to this motor encoding. Central to the encoding of actions during enactment, for them, is the aspect that for tasks to be performed, they must be planned and their enactment must be initiated. The fundamental difference from the assumptions of Bäckman and Nilsson is that, in Bäckman and Nilsson's opinion, all sensory and motor features contribute to the enactment effect. In Engelkamp and Zimmer's opinion, however, only the motor features contribute to the enactment effect.

Generally speaking, Engelkamp and Zimmer distinguish three phases for encoding: a sensory, a conceptual, and a motor phase. The sensory encoding processes rely decisively upon stimulus modality. Verbal stimuli induce verbal-sensory encoding processes and activate representations in the verbal system or mental lexicon. Engelkamp and Zimmer (1985) call these representations word nodes. Pictorial stimuli induce correspondingly visual-sensory encoding processes. They activate so-called picture nodes. The meaning connected with picture and word nodes is represented in a conceptual system. The meaning is activated from word or picture nodes. The representations for the meanings are designated as concepts. When an action phrase such as "lift up the pen" is read to a subject, it leads to the activation of the word nodes and subsequently to the activation of the concepts for this phrase. If the subject carries out the action described in the phrase, motor encoding takes place and a motor programme is activated additionally. This means, the motor movements characterised by the action (e.g. "pen lifting") are planned and programmed. This programme is then finally carried out (e.g. Engelkamp & Zimmer, 1983, 1985).

It is clear that for Engelkamp and Zimmer the enactment effect is attributed to motor encoding. Since they attribute the enactment effect to motor encoding (and not to sensory—for example to visual-imaginal encoding processes), they did not use any real objects in their experiments. Instead, the actions were to be carried out symbolically, using imaginary objects. At first, they concentrated their experimental efforts on proving that the enactment effect actually was based upon motor processes, not on visual-sensory processes. For this they utilised the paradigm of dual tasks as well. However, they used it to demonstrate structural interference rather than central interference (cf. Chapter 2).

The paradigm of selective structural interference is based on the assumption that the processing operations within a system reciprocally interfere with each other more than processes from different systems. The assumption of different types of representation (word nodes, picture nodes, concepts, motor programmes) implies that the different types form separate systems and that the representations of one type are more similar to each other than to the representations of other types. Accordingly, picture nodes are more similar to one another than are picture nodes and word nodes. Analogous to this, it is true that motor programmes are more homogeneous with each other than motor programmes and picture nodes. For each representation type, a system is assumed in which the units are represented and in which these units are processed. If motor programmes are critical for the enactment effect, then processing additional motor information in direct temporal proximity should selectively impair the enactment effect. In this case, retention after SPTs should be more impaired after additional motor processing than after additional visual processing. The processing of additional information was realised within the dual task paradigm.

A series of such structural interference experiments were carried out in the first half of the 1980s. Although in a first experiment Zimmer, Engelkamp, and Sieloff (1984, Exp. 1) observed a disordinal (cross-over) interaction for SPTs and EPTs and type of interference (motor, visual), they could not replicate this pattern in further experiments. The main difference between this first and the other experiments was that subjects in the visual learning condition no longer perceived the experimenter performing the actions (EPTs), but instead imagined someone else performing the actions. I have no convincing explanation for this inconsistent finding, and I will not deal with this inconsistency any further. I have mentioned this first experiment mainly because it motivated further experimentation.

One central question was whether similar selective interference effects as in Exp. 1 of Zimmer et al. (1984) could also be observed when the actions of another person were only visually imagined. The interference should continue to be visual-sensory and motor. When actions are imagined, the picture nodes are no longer activated bottom-up, as in observing actions, but top-down instead. According to experiments of visual-verbal selective interference it can be assumed that interference processes arise here as well. Whether the units of the visual system are activated bottom-up or top-down should be irrelevant for the selective visual interference.

This question was investigated with very similar material in very similar procedures by Saltz and Donnenwerth-Nolan (1981) and by Zimmer et al. (1984). In both experiments subjects learned simple action sentences (such as "The quiz-master draws the lottery ticket"). In one condition, the subjects put themselves into the role of the agent and symbolically (without any real objects) performed the tasks (enactment condition). In another condition, the subjects were to visualise how the actor of the sentence would perform the task (visual-imagery condition). The motor interference task in both experiments consisted of the subjects being required to perform body-related tasks such as "lift your arm". The visual interference condition by Saltz and Donnenwerth-Nolan (1981) consisted of static pictures of actions that the subjects were supposed to remember. In this condition, Zimmer et al. had their subjects remember video spots of events (not actions; e.g. the rotating spool of a cassette). Learning items and interference items were presented alternately in both cases. Retention was tested in both studies by using the subject of the sentence as a cue. In both experiments an important inter-action between learning and disrupting conditions was observed. Never-theless, the findings were partially different. Saltz and Donnenwerth-Nolan observed a disordinal interaction. Zimmer et al. observed a selective inter-ference only under the motor learning condition. The performance after visual-imaginal learning did not differ after visual and motor interference (Fig. 3.2).

In addition to a score for the entire sentence, Zimmer et al. calculated separate scores for the recall of the object words and verbs. These showed the interaction effect for the verbs, but not for the nouns. Only learning through enactment was interfered with selectively by enactment.

The inconsistent results for the visual-imaginal condition in the studies of Saltz and Donnenwerth-Nolan (1981) and Zimmer et al. (1984) and the differential effect for nouns and verbs for Zimmer and Engelkamp (1985) were reason enough to explore the possible causes through a further experiment. The main difference in this experiment from the previous experiment was that the learning material for visual imagery was adapted to the contents of the visual interference material. All of the other conditions were the same. In other words, action sentences were learned by enactment and event sentences were learned by visual imagery. The visual interference once again consisted of video spots of events, the motor interference of body-related actions.

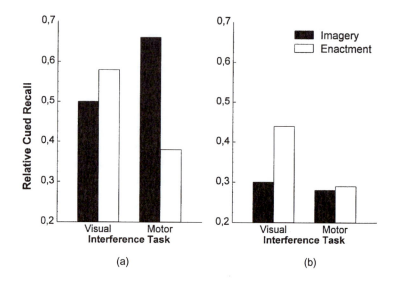

FIG. 3.2.   Cued recall as a function of the encoding condition (imagery, enactment) and of the visual and motor interference tasks (according to data from (a) Saltz & Donnenwerth-Nolan, 1981, and (b) Zimmer, Engelkamp, & Sieloff, 1984, Exp. 2).

Once again, the imagined sentences were recalled equally well after both visual and motor interference. The enacted action sentences were again recalled distinctly more poorly after motor interference than after visual interference. As in the experiment reported previously, separate analyses of verbs and nouns showed a clear interaction effect for verbs and no inter-action effect for nouns. The results are illustrated in Fig. 3.3.

Zimmer and Engelkamp (1985) saw the fact that the results in visual imagery had not changed in comparison to those from the first experiment as proof that these results are not artifacts. The fact that they are limited to verbs led them to assume that the motor components include the visual components of motion. Whereas events, that is foreign motions, do not disrupt ones own motions, the latter, that is motor enactment, include a general movement component and therefore disrupt visually imagined motions as well. The fact that Saltz and Donnenwerth-Nolan (1981) had also observed selective interference for the visual-imaginal condition might be due to the fact that they had suppressed the movement components in the visually imagined condition by the instruction to imagine the outward appearance of the actor as well as the situation by visualisation. This interpretation was supported by the fact that the grammatical subjects of events were recalled much better than the verbs, but also better than the grammatical subjects of actions. Interference through movement had little

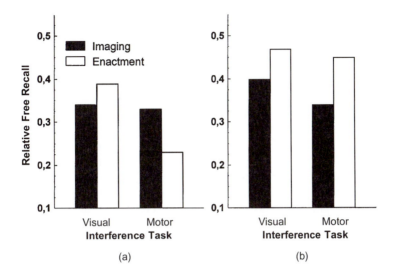

FIG. 3.3.   Free recall of (a) verbs and (b) nouns as a function of encoding conditions (imagery, enactment) and the visual and motor interference tasks (according to data from Engelkamp & Zimmer, 1985, Exp. 1).

effect on them. This interpretation was also supported by an investigation by Cohen (1989b).

In a further experiment, Zimmer and Engelkamp (1985, Exp. 2) investigated whether motor processes also could be activated without actual movements. They assumed that the comparison of the course of movement in two motor tasks presupposed the activation of their motor programmes. In this experiment as well, sentences about events were learned by visual imagery and action phrases by enactment. As a motor interference task, the subjects received two action phrases one after the other and were to determine whether the two tasks had a similar course of movement, for example "to polish the car" and "to wipe off the table", or "to make a fist" and "to squeeze out a sponge". The visual interference tasks were constructed analogously. Here the subjects had to compare two movement patterns from a beam of light presented one after the other. Again a selective interference effect was only observed after SPT learning. The retention performance was poorer under the motor interference condition than under the condition of visual interference. The visually imaged events, however, again were recalled equally well under both interference conditions.

These experiments seem to suggest that motor programmes can not only be activated by plain motor behaviour, but also by the internal simulation of these actions. Such a simulation ought to take place when the task requires the processing of information that is in the motor programme. This is the case if the course of movements must be assessed.

The assumption that tasks requiring the assessment of how the movements are carried out contain motor programmes was also investigated by Engelkamp and Zimmer (1984). In this experiment they argued: If the sequence of movements in two tasks is to be compared, that is, if it must be assessed that, for example, the action of "turning a crank" is similar to "mixing dough", then the corresponding motor programme must be activated to resolve the task. This should imply two things. First, in particular tasks, it should be possible to activate motor programmes even without enactment instructions and without the actual performance of the actions. Second, it should be possible to read this motor information from the motor programme and transfer it into the conceptual system from which the information can be put out. The last process listed here ought to cost time. This amount of time should be reduced if the motor programme had already been activated by the tasks being performed.

Engelkamp and Zimmer (1984) tested this assumption. They presented the subjects successively with two action phrases and instructed them to judge if the movement pattern of the actions was similar or dissimilar. The second action phrase was always presented visually. The amount of time from the beginning of the display of the second phrase to the time of decision was measured through the pressing of a key. The processing of the first phrase was varied. It was always presented acoustically and was either to be repeated out loud or the appropriate actions were to be performed. Only the performance of the action should activate the motor programme and provide the information on the movement pattern. In contrast, the verbal repetition should tend to prevent this programme activation. Further, the second programme should be partially pre-activated through the performance of the first task. The comparison of the programme and the output over the conceptual system should be the same under both conditions. Half of the phrase pairs had similar movement patterns and half of the pairs contained different movement patterns.

It was found that the similarity of two movement patterns was judged faster than their dissimilarity, and, more important, performance of the first action led to a shorter judgement time than verbal repetition of the phrase.

According to Engelkamp and Zimmer (1984), these results substantiate, first of all, that the activation of a motor programme can also be triggered without performance of an action, through tasks that require the motor information. The same logic had also been applied with regard to the activation of picture nodes (e.g. Glass, Millen, Beck, & Eddy, 1985; Zimmer, 1988). There it was also assumed that the solving of particular tasks, for example the verification of the sentence "A tractor has larger back wheels than front wheels" requires the activation of picture nodes.

For Engelkamp and Zimmer, the results, secondly, substantiate that the performance of an action makes such movement information available. This is manifested in the shorter judgement time after enactment of the first task in comparison to verbally repeating the action phrase.

Nevertheless, it can be objected that the judgement is based on visual-imagery information, and not on motor information. In other words, it could also be that performance of the action only makes visual-imagery information available. To challenge this argument, the experiment was replicated in two versions (Engelkamp, 1985). In one version, the actions of the first phrase had to be visually imagined or to be enacted. In the other version, the phrases were to be repeated or their actions to be visually imagined. Through this it was shown that a shorter judgement time appeared in comparison to verbal repetition only after enactment and not under any of the visual-imagery instructions. The cause for the shorter time must be sought in the specific motor information which was made available by enactment.

Engelkamp and Zimmer (1984) therefore held it as probable that the motor information affected retention as well. This assumption was supported by the experiments on selective interference. These experiments demonstrated that the enactment effect was based on motor information. It was shown in every experiment that recall performance after enactment was selectively disrupted by an additional motor task and it was shown that the enactment effect was considerably reduced, or even reversed, under conditions of motor interference. In other words, in some experiments the actions were recalled less well after motor encoding than after visual or visual-imagery encoding. In every case, however, motor interference resulted in the disappearance of the enactment effect.

Contrary to the expectation, under visual imagery conditions there was no selective interference. Recall performance under visual interference was here equal to the recall level under motor interference. This finding might be due to the fact that enactment activates not only motor processes but also visual-sensory processes.

Unfortunately, Engelkamp and Zimmer did not use any interference-free control conditions in their experiments. Moreover, they ignored the considerations on central interference in their experiments. Because of this, the interpretation of their data must remain preliminary.

ENACTMENT AS ITEM-SPECIFIC ENCODING

As already explained in Chapter 2, Einstein and Hunt (1980) and Hunt and Einstein (1981) drew the attention of memory researchers to item-specific and relational encoding processes.

Some interesting questions can be asked with regard to learning action phrases through enactment. Does item-specific encoding or relational encoding tend to improve through enactment in comparison to listening? Or do both types of encoding improve? These questions had, however, not yet been posed during the early phase of the investigation into recollection of self-performed tasks. Nevertheless, I want to touch upon this point because the distinction between item-specific and relational information plays a major role in the multimodal memory theory, which is discussed in the next chapter. More or less all researchers assume that enactment improves item-specific encoding (Bäckman & Nilsson, 1985; Engelkamp, 1988; Helstrup, 1986; Knopf, 1991; Kormi-Nouri, 1994; Mohr, Engelkamp, & Zimmer, 1989; Nyberg, 1993; Saltz & Donnenwerth-Nolan, 1981; Zimmer, 1984).

A first indication that item-specific encoding could be critical for the enactment effect has already been given by Cohen (1981, p. 278). He ascertained that memory models for verbal learning often accentuate organisational processes (e.g. Anderson & Bower, 1972). If the subjects encoded actions by enactment in the way that they reported, then enactment would not stimulate organisational processes. According to the statements of subjects, attention was drawn to every single action only at the moment of performance. In other words, the self-reports provided by the subjects spoke in favour of independent encoding of the individual actions through enactment.

Saltz (Saltz & Dixon, 1982; Saltz & Donnenwerth-Nolan, 1981) had also emphasised this aspect early on. In his opinion, an additional feature is encoded through enactment, and this feature improves the ability to distinguish memory traces after enactment (cf. also Helstrup, 1986; Saltz, 1988). In contrast to Cohen (1981), Saltz, like Engelkamp and Zimmer (1985), viewed the motor component as important here. For Engelkamp and Zimmer, good item-specific information after enactment is based primarily on the motor component. Bäckman and Nilsson (e.g. 1985) consider rich multimodal encoding as critical for good retention after enactment and do not exclude good item-specific encoding. They alone additionally assume that this rich multimodal encoding also facilitates relational encoding.

In this respect, they differ from Engelkamp and Zimmer (e.g. Engelkamp, 1988; Zimmer & Engelkamp, 1989a). They assume that encoding after enactment and listening differ in regard to item-specific information, but not to relational information. Here it may simply be recorded that Zimmer and Engelkamp (1989a) and Zimmer (1991) were not able to observe any difference in organisational measures as an indicator for relational encoding between the learning of tasks by listening and enactment. Bäckman and Nilsson (1984) and Bäckman et al. (1986) did observe such a difference, however.

Kormi-Nouri (1994) additionally suggests that the item-specific infor-mation, which is made available through enactment, is conceptual (see also Knopf, 1991). He considers the assumption of motor processes as being unnecessary.

Nyberg (1993) lies closer to the position of Engelkamp and Zimmer with regard to item-specific information. He attributes the emphasis to the motor components and views the sensory object qualities as rather irrelevant for the enactment effect. I will examine these differences and controversies more closely in Chapter 5. At this point the following should be recorded:

1. The assumption that SPTs increase item-specific information in comparison to listening to action phrases is shared by practically all researchers.
2. This increase in item-specific information through enactment is either attributed, depending on the author, to conceptual, nonverbal sensory, or nonverbal motor information, or the type of information remains unspecified.
3. There is no uniform point of view with regard to relational encoding. While Bäckman and Nilsson assume that enactment also improves relational information in comparison with listening, Engelkamp and Zimmer assume that relational encoding does not differ between lis-tening and enactment.

As unanimous as the authors may be with regard to the explanation of the enactment effect by good item-specific encoding, experiments have brought little substantiation (cf. Engelkamp & Cohen, 1991). It proves to be extremely difficult to verify this assumption convincingly. Nevertheless, the following conclusions favour better item-specific encoding of tasks through enactment than through listening.

Although Zimmer and Engelkamp (1989a) were not able to observe any difference in relational encoding after listening and enactment, they found a distinct enactment effect (cf. also Zimmer, 1991). Further, an enactment effect also appeared in Bäckman et al. (1986), where relational encoding was difficult because of an attention-demanding interference task (Exp. 1) or because of the items were unrelated (Exp. 2). Similarly, in Exp. 1 of Zimmer and Engelkamp (1989a), the enactment effect was no smaller for unrelated items than for related items. These findings speak in favour of the assumption that better item-specific information is available after enactment than after listening.

Above and beyond that, the enactment effect did not show up in some cases of recall, but was always present in recognition memory. For example, the enactment effect was absent in recall when, for various reasons, reten-tion in the control situation was already very good (e.g. Helstrup, 1989a;

Knopf, 1989; Mohr et al., 1989; Zimmer & Engelkamp, in press). I know of no experiment in which the enactment effect was not observed in a recognition test. Beyond this it was shown that it is very difficult to reduce the good recognition performance through enactment. This emerges particularly impressively from one investigation by Engelkamp, Zimmer, and Biegelmann (1993). They used various methods without success to make recognition more difficult.

Zimmer (1991) applied a method for learning tasks that had been introduced by Rabinowitz, Mandler, and Barsalou (1979). This method was based upon the "generation-recognition" model of recollection. The subjects studied categorically structured lists. After the list presentation, free recall took place. Afterwards, the subjects received the category labels and generated all of the examples that occurred to them for these categories. Finally, they were to cross off which of the generated words appeared in the original list. This procedure allowed generating and recognising to be separated. With this procedure, Zimmer was able to observe the following: (1) After listening and enactment, a comparably equal amount of examples were generated. (2) After enactment, more of the items were list items. That is to say, more "old" items were generated after enactment than after listening. (3) More importantly, the percentage of the "old" items generated that were also recognised as being "old" was also greater after enactment than listening. Looking at the proportion of the "old" items generated that were also recognised as "old" as an indicator for the richness of the item-specific information, it is shown that this is greater after enactment than after listening. Nevertheless, it might be possible that exactly as many "old" items were recognised as being "old" after VTs as after SPTs if the same number of "old" items had been produced after listening as after enactment.

It remains to be recorded that the various findings tend to speak in favour of better item-specific information after enactment than after listening. The situation with regard to relational information is unclear.

CHAPTER FOUR

Theoretical integration I: Actions as described by the multimodal theory

The early attempts to explain the advantage of enactment for retention were characterised by the fact that the majority concentrated on one cause. Cohen (e.g. 1985) concentrated on the aspect of automatic encoding, whereas Engelkamp and Zimmer (1985) concentrated on the aspect of motor encoding. The same may almost be stated of Saltz (e.g. Saltz & Donnenwerth-Nolan, 1981). Only Bäckman and Nilsson (e.g. 1984, 1985) considered the matter from a wider angle.

I would now like to show that all three of the dimensions considered decisive (multimodality, item-specific/relational, and automatic/controlled) can be integrated in a single approach. The multimodal memory theory (Engelkamp, 1990) represents such an approach. It permits the findings reported to be explained within a single theoretical framework.

THE MULTIMODAL MEMORY THEORY

The multimodal memory theory can only be referred to briefly here (for detailed information see Engelkamp, 1990; and Engelkamp & Zimmer, 1994b). The theory basically deals with the differentiation between modality-specific entry systems, which all have access to a common conceptual system, and modality-specific output systems, which can all be controlled from the conceptual system but which can also be controlled directly from particular entry systems without going via the conceptual system (Fig. 4.1). In the present context, I shall confine myself, in the field of nonverbal

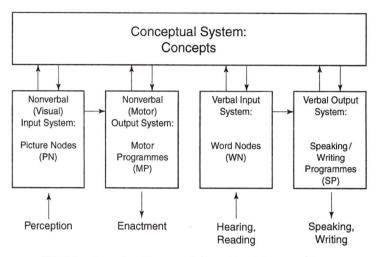

FIG. 4.1. General architecture of the multimodal memory theory.

stimulus processing, to visual stimuli. The system assumption postulates that processing in the individual subsystems can to a large extent take place independently of processing in other subsystems and that direct links do not exist between all subsystems. I prefer to speak simply of systems instead of code systems.

For the sake of simplicity and better communicability I call the memory representations in the visual entry system "picture nodes" (PN), those in the nonverbal motor output system "motor programmes" (MP), those in the verbal entry system "word nodes" (WN) (I choose to ignore the division into visual/acoustic presentation modalities here), and those in the verbal output system "speaking/writing programmes" (I use the shared abbreviation SP here). Only a visual entry system is presented here. However, it should be emphasised that this system is itself complex and must be differentiated (cf. Engelkamp, 1995c; Zimmer, 1995b). In the present context the processing of static object stimuli and of dynamic motion stimuli is to be especially differentiated, whereby in the present context action motions are of particular interest.

With regard to memory experiments in which intentional learning (I ignore incidental learning) and explicit recall are investigated, I make the basic postulation that the conceptual system is of major meaning in processing. Under these premises, words set off processes in the verbal entry system and pictures, objects and events set off processes in the visual entry system (here it should be taken into consideration that there are analogous systems for acoustic, tactile, smell, and taste stimuli, cf. Wippich, 1990a, 1990b, 1991; Wippich & Wagner, 1989), which activate in the conceptual system corresponding concepts associated with them. From here a verbal or nonverbal action is planned, as required, which then sets off processes in the verbal or motor output system. In other words, the output systems can be involved in learning—but this is not compulsory. As a rule no overt motor reaction is required in the learning phase. As Craik and Lockhart (1972), I consider the processes in the conceptual system as being the most important for episodic retention. Furthermore, I assume that in explicit retention the sensory processes are only effective within the context of conceptual processes. In other words, the explicit recall of sensory properties is always the recall of such properties as part of stimuli that are interpreted categorically, that is as part of concepts. Without recalling a concept it is not possible to remember sensory properties which are connected to the concept in an explicit test. On the other hand, if I explicitly recall a concept, this recall is supported by the sensory properties connected to it, that is the recall of a concept, for example an apple, which has been seen, also depends on its appearance.

Analogous assumptions are true of the output systems. Their retention efficiency is equally dependent on simultaneous conceptual processing. Motor processes which take place in the learning phase are only retention efficient within the context of conceptual encoding too. In other words, recall of an action concept, for example that I have combed my hair, depends on the movement performed.

At this point it is appropriate to state more clearly what is meant by sensory and motor processes, or rather, what specific information picture nodes and motor programmes contain. Since it is assumed that explicit retention is not restricted to recalling abstract meanings, but also includes the sensory aspects of the learning episode, the specific sensory information is dependent on the specific properties of each stimulus to be learned and on the modality of its processing. If we take the visual processing modality, then for static objects sensory information would be shape, colour, size, orientation, texture, etc. With visually perceived actions it would be the sensory information on the process of the movement, its form and speed and the parts of the body involved. With self-performed actions it would be motor information. Motor information means the way in which the action was performed. When we remember that we did perform an action, this means that we can differentiate whether we only intended to perform an action, only imagined doing so, or whether we really did perform it. It does not, however, mean that we also remember *how* we performed the action. This last recollection includes information on the way it was performed, such as form and speed. Since these aspects (at least in part) are planned before the action is performed, then part of the motor information should also be available when the action has been planned but not yet performed. So it is important to differentiate between an action being planned and being performed.

The assumptions regarding sensory and motor retention efficiency are partially based on the fact that we can recall episodes in all their sensory and motor richness. In our subjective experience—for example when we recall a scene of the previous evening—we recall not only abstract meanings, but also the sensory qualities. Similarly, we recall the motor qualities of climbing a tree.

It follows from these assumptions that although both sensory and motor processes exert a positive influence on explicit retention, each of these influences should be independent of each other. The sensory processes set off by seeing an object, for example, can occur without a motor reaction being linked to them. The processes linked to reaction, such as naming or describing the object, can, in turn, ensue relatively independently of perceiving the object.

It is clear that the assumptions on the multimodality of encoding extend beyond those of Bäckman and Nilsson (e.g. 1985) and of Engelkamp and Zimmer (e.g. 1985), they specify them and thus integrate them in a wider framework. Bäckman and Nilsson's postulations are specified insofar that the various different pieces of sensory and motor information are independent in their effectiveness on retention. This means, for example, that the retention effects of perceiving an object used in an action should be independent of that of perceiving the action itself, and the effect of this should in turn be independent of that of performing the action oneself (see also Meltzoff, 1990). Only the latter is an enactment effect in the real sense, and this is what Engelkamp and Zimmer (1985) emphasise.

Engelkamp and Zimmer's postulations (e.g. 1985) are specified in particular in that a distinction is made in motor information between information which becomes available through planning the action and information which is only made available through the action being performed. In addition, a distinction is made in the latter case between the information that an action has been performed and how it was performed.

In this multimodal model it seems reasonable to regard all the processes involved in encoding an event as item-specific information. In the example of naming an object this would mean that the sensory processes of perceiving the object, the process of interpreting its meaning and the motor process of producing the name together make up the item-specific encoding. In other words, not only conceptual but also sensory and motor processes can contribute to item-specific encoding. The item-specific information involved in naming an object is shown in Fig. 4.2.

The good quality of the item-specific encoding for action phrases when the action is performed compared to when the action phrase is heard results from the fact that as a rule listening to a phrase only leads to the activation of the word node and of the action concept, whereas performing additionally activates a motor programme. The basic assumption that any additional

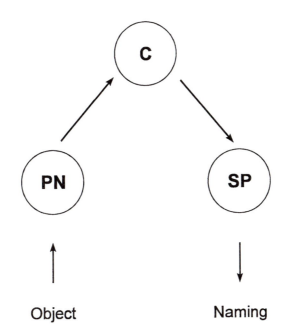

FIG. 4.2.   Illustration of the item-specific encoding for naming an object. PN stands for picture node, C for concept, and SP for speaking programme.

aspect encoded for an item has a positive effect on retention is to be found in almost all propositions that try to explain the enactment effect (e.g. Bäckman & Nilsson, 1984, 1985; Engelkamp & Zimmer, 1983, 1985; Saltz, 1988). Here it is stated more precisely in that the decisive encoding aspect for the enactment effect is considered to be that of the programme activation.

Where do the relational processes occur in such a model? The answer to this question is simple: Relational encoding processes are confined to the conceptual system. The grounds for this answer are complicated, so I would like to go back somewhat. A suitable starting point for the argument would be semantic priming effects and models of spreading activation in the semantic system (e.g. Anderson, 1985). Words are more easily processed if a prime word semantically related to the target word is offered shortly before presentation of the latter. To give an example: if the word "milk" is to be recognised, then less time is needed if, for example, 200msec beforehand the word "cow" was shown than if the word "house" was shown. This processing advantage for a word that has been preceded by one similar in meaning as opposed to one dissimilar in meaning is explained by spreading activation in the conceptual system. The process of spreading activation is demonstrated in Fig. 4.3.

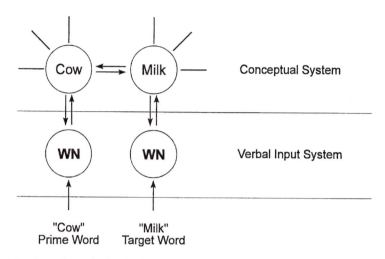

FIG. 4.3.   Spreading activation in the semantic priming paradigm. WN stands for word node.

At the same time as a concept is activated in the conceptual system its semantic environment is automatically activated for a certain period of time. If someone hears the word "garden", then with and besides the concept of garden they also activate knowledge closely related to "garden". To a certain degree they co-activate concepts such as lawn, patio, flowers, weeds, etc. This co-activation of associated knowledge ensues automatically and it prepares one for the perception of probable stimuli (cf. Hoffmann, 1993).

The spreading of activation in the sensory systems is different. It has other, temporal properties. If, for example, the word "milk" is presented, then it may well seem sensible to activate word nodes which are pronounced (or written) similarly, such as "middle" or "million", as long as the word remains unrecognised (e.g. Humphreys, Evett, Quinlan, & Besner, 1987). It makes little sense, however, to keep these words activated once the word "milk" has been recognised. The identification of the word "milk" consists precisely in differentiating it from the others. This occurs by excluding, that is inhibiting, the alternatives (e.g. McClelland & Rumelhart, 1981). If this did not happen then there would be the danger that the meanings associated with the competing words could also be activated, and this would impede the "understanding" of the word presented. Even more convincing is the necessity of mutual inhibition in motor programmes. If, for example, the word "milk" is to be enunciated, it would be very distracting if other articulation programmes for words such as "million" or "middle" were to compete.

Another difference in spreading of activation in the sensory and motor systems on the one hand and in the conceptual system on the other is that in the conceptual system activation spreads between concepts, whereas in the sensory and motor systems the activation spread consists rather of a certain system first being activated throughout large areas and then everything being inhibited except a small section corresponding to one node or programme. If similar nodes or programmes are activated shortly after each other in the latter systems, then the ability to differentiate them suffers because sections will be activated that overlap each other.

Hence, the multimodal theory expects a spread of activation, lasting for the moment when a stimulus is recognised, to occur in the conceptual network alone and only to be of assistance to encoding here. This spread first occurs during learning. It promotes relational encoding wherever semantically related words occur in sufficient temporal proximity to each other, because their concepts are activated simultaneously. It also occurs during recall, where it promotes the process of generating concepts thus relationally encoded.

The situation is different with regard to links that still have to be created between (as yet unconnected) action concepts. In such a case, it is to be expected that performing actions makes it difficult to form new associations in the conceptual system. It is assumed that this is because planning and performing an action forces concentration on the information relevant to the action, more so than listening action phrases or perceiving actions. This concentration on information relevant to the action is a prerequisite for the undistracted performance of actions. Ignoring it would lead to errors. The positive consequence of this focusing on information relevant to the action is the excellent quality of the item-specific encoding. The negative consequence is the poor quality of the relational encoding of unrelated actions (Engelkamp, 1991a, 1995b). In order to distinguish this relational encoding from the encoding of concept links already existing before the experiment, I call the former episodic-relational and the latter categorical-relational. "Categorical" stands for all kinds of systematic pre-experimental links between concepts.

The successive activation of nodes or programmes (e.g. upon occurrence of acoustically similar words) tends rather to have a negative effect. It makes it more difficult to distinguish the memory representations because they overlap structurally. This overlapping occurs both in the sensory and the motor systems. Since we are considering the memory trace of individual stimuli here I ascribe these overlapping effects to item-specific encoding.

If we assume that categorical-relational encoding in the conceptual system is mainly based on the automatic spreading of activation of pre-experimental links in this system and that more or less the same concepts are activated upon listening and performing action phrases, then categorical-relational encoding should not differentiate between the two conditions.

These assumptions expand and specify those of Bäckman and Nilsson (e.g. 1985) and of Engelkamp and Zimmer (e.g. 1985) with regard to the concept of relational information in two ways: in relating to pre-experimental links in the conceptual system (categorical-relational information) on the one hand and to the concept links that are to be created in the learning episode (episodic-relational information) on the other. It further specifies the concept by emphasising the function of relational information in the conceptual system as opposed to that in the sensory and motor systems. In these systems the similarity of representations activated shortly after each other should rather have a negative effect on retention. As I have already said, I ascribe these effects to item-specific encoding.

As far as the differentiation between automatic and controlled processes is concerned I make the following postulations based on the multimodal memory theory. First, encoding processes are considered automatic if they occur necessarily with a given stimulus and a given task. When a visually perceived object is to be named, for example, the corresponding picture node, concept, and speaking programme are necessarily activated. If the label of an object was to be read aloud, only the word node and the speaking programme would be activated of necessity. The concept would probably be co-activated due to the habitualised tendency to want to understand words. The picture node, however, would not automatically be activated. Similarly, upon instructions to perform an action phrase the motor programme would necessarily be activated in addition to the word node and the concept, but would not automatically be activated upon instructions to listen to the phrase. Second, it is assumed that pre-experimental connections between concepts that are to be learned are automatically activated. Third, encoding processes are considered to be controlled (or strategic) if the person encoding employs them voluntarily. The strategic processes can be started off by self-instruction (e.g. if a person actively tries to create links between stimuli) or by instructions given by the experimenter. These would be the kind of instructions which for the most part leave it to the test person to form the concrete encoding processes (e.g. "Make up a story using the words in the list"). Instructions to perform simple actions (e.g. "pick up the pencil") leave little room for creativity in this respect. They tend to set off automatic encoding processes. Fourth, it is necessary to differentiate from the matter of automatic vs. controlled encoding the aspect of conscious experience. The encoding processes can lead to conscious perceptions, which differ in their richness. I postulate that verbal stimuli set off less rich conscious experiences than nonverbal stimuli, since the former are more abstract and require concretisation. Furthermore, I postulate that performing actions sets off particularly rich conscious experiences. These account for the good retention of actions performed that do not require voluntary encoding processes.

These latter postulations modify the assumptions of Cohen (e.g. 1983) and of Bäckman et al. (1986). They differentiate these positions through the distinction between strategic and automatic processes on the one hand and their effect on conscious encoding on the other. The aspect that automatic processes can also go along with conscious experience is of particular meaning. Expanding these assumptions in this way allows us to expect good explicit retention even with automatic encoding.

Differentiating automatic and controlled encoding implies that controlled processes can be disturbed if they are also needed for secondary tasks. This is *central* interference (cf. also Norman & Bobrow, 1975). It is to be distinguished from *structural* interference, which occurs independently of whether the respective processes are controlled or automatic. It is caused by the same (structural) system being used several times in quick succession. This double usage leads to a decrease in the efficiency of the encoding processes, caused primarily by the fact that processes in the same system are masking each other and thus making the traces they leave in the memory more difficult to distinguish.

The distinction between structural and central interference modifies and integrates the proposals on interference put forward by Bäckman et al. (1986) on the one hand and by Zimmer and Engelkamp (e.g. 1985) on the other.

EXPLANATIONS OF FINDINGS ON THE ENACTMENT EFFECT AND NEW PREDICTIONS BASED ON THE MULTIMODAL MEMORY THEORY

In this next section the findings on recalling self-performed actions detailed in Chapter 3 are considered in the light of the multimodal memory theory and some predictions arising from this theory are discussed.

Effects of Multimodal Encoding

The differentiation between sensory and motor processes and within the sensory processes between object and action processing corresponds closely to the proposals put forward by Bäckman and Nilsson (e.g. 1984, 1985). There are at least two significant differences, however. The first relates to the assumption that the modality-specific systems are subordinated to the conceptual system, and in the context of explicit recall modality-specific memory traces are tied to conceptual memory traces. In other words, in explicit recall modality-specific memory traces can only take effect together with, that is in the context of, conceptual information.

The second aspect where the multimodal theory differs from Bäckman and Nilsson (e.g. 1984, 1985) relates to their postulation that the enactment effect is caused by the accumulated effects of encoding the various sensory and motor stimulus aspects (such as colour, texture, weight of the object of the action, and type of movement). According to the multimodal theory, these aspects can all contribute to recall performance but are not all specific to enactment. In my opinion, the critical question regarding the enactment effect is: Which of the processes that promote retention only occur in the context of actions if an action is self-performed? In other words, the point of interest is which encoding processes are enactment-specific. Unfortunately, the findings of Chapter 3 that prove the enactment effect are unsuitable for answering this question because the experiments were not sophisticated enough.

How should experiments be carried out so that the causes of the enactment effect may be ascertained more precisely? In order to clarify the basis of the enactment effect, all the processes that occur under the performance condition as well as the respective control conditions should be kept constant as far as possible. Here further experiments are desirable.

The multimodal memory theory also predicts findings on structural interference. One problem always facing system theories is that better retention can nearly always be explained by the assumption of conceptual encoding processes of varyingly high quality (e.g. Knopf, 1992,1995). The most convincing data for a system approach are presented by structural interference effects. The ideal case here is considered to be disordinal interaction. For the distinction between a visual-sensory and a motor system this would mean that retention following visual encoding (e.g. upon seeing an action) is more strongly impaired by a "visual" secondary task than by a "motor" secondary task, and that the opposite happens with retention following motor encoding (e.g. upon performing an action). Here the "motor" secondary task should impair retention more than the "visual" one.

However, experiments by Zimmer et al. (1984) and by Zimmer and Engelkamp (1985) where the same interaction pattern had been expected produced different findings. Although in several experiments retention following enactment did produce selective interference caused by a motor secondary task, yet as far as the visual-imaginal encoding of actions was concerned, no differential interference in retention was caused either by a "motor" or a "visual" secondary task. The positive aspect of this result is that selective motor interference following enactment was still observed. This coincides with the assumptions of the multimodal theory. The problem is the absence of selective interference after "visual" encoding.

A possible explanation following from the multimodal models is as follows: Although with Zimmer et al. (1984) and Zimmer and Engelkamp (1985) both motor interference and encoding in the main task always involved the verbal entry system too (the phrases were always presented verbally), the visual interference task was nonverbal, that is the subjects only saw video clips of events, for example. Since the main task included the verbal system even in the "imagine" task (phrases were presented), the motor secondary task while imagining could have been "verbally" distracting (but not "visually") and the "visual" interference task could have been "visually" distracting (but not "verbally"). In this way visual and verbal interference while imagining could have balanced each other out. The selective interference effect upon instructions to imagine an action observed by Saltz and Donnenwerth-Nolan (1981), who also used a purely visual secondary task, seems to refute this. However, they used standing pictures, which could have promoted implicit naming. Besides, these authors used relatively complex encoding instructions in the main task.

To summarise: Selective motor interference supports the system theory, while the findings on visual interference do not allow clear interpretation because the experimental controls were insufficient. The multimodal theory makes it clear that conditions for encoding in the main and the secondary tasks must be controlled more differentiatingly. Thus it must be ensured that the encoding processes in the main and secondary tasks remain constant except for one component. This goes especially for visual encoding. If visual selective interference shall be demonstrated, not only must it be ensured that the verbal encoding processes in the main and the secondary tasks remain constant, it must also be taken into consideration that the visual system itself consists of subsystems which in part work independently. Thus, one visual subsystem could be responsible for perceiving static objects and another for perceiving dynamic, that is moving stimuli. Any change of these components from the main task to the secondary task influences the observed performance. These considerations show not only that the experiments reported on were based on theoretical ideas which were too simple, but also that it is extremely difficult to carry out well-controlled interference experiments.

Finally, it should be mentioned that the experiments on motor preactivation (Engelkamp, 1985; Engelkamp & Zimmer, 1984) support the assumptions of a motor system and the fact that it is different to a verbal and a visual system.

The multimodal memory theory not only allows the explanation and evaluation of existing findings on multimodal encoding, it also suggests further hypotheses and new experiments. Here are some of the hypotheses:

1. Recall of actions observed should differ from that of actions performed, because in each case different systems are involved in encoding.
2. For the same reason, perceiving real objects should improve retention compared to a control condition without real objects, and this effect should be independent of the enactment effect.

3. Planning an action should lead to poorer recall than planning and performing an action, because the latter condition includes planning the action. Both conditions should improve retention compared with a listening condition, where no motor processes take place.
4. Structural interference effects should not only be shown in the dual task paradigm but also via the variation with system-specific similarities of stimuli, since stimuli that are structurally similar are less easily distinguished from each other.

Experiments dealing with these hypotheses will be reported in Chapter 5.

Effects of Item-specific and Relational Encoding

As far as item-specific encoding is concerned, all researchers involved agree that it is positively influenced by enactment. There is less agreement on the influence of enactment on relational encoding processes.

The opinions on item-specific encoding differ, however, on the question of whether the positive influence of enactment (and item-specific encoding in general) is of a conceptual nature (e.g. Knopf, 1991), whether it relates to multimodal (both sensory and motor) encoding processes (e.g. Bäckman & Nilsson, 1984, 1985), or primarily to motor processes (Zimmer & Engelkamp, 1985). According to the multimodal theory an important cause for the high level of retention of actions performed lies in the quality of its motor item-specific encoding. A problem in the motor explanation, however, is that it is hardly possible to decide, on the basis of the findings reported in Chapter 3, which parts of item-specific encoding are particularly promoted by enactment. It has become clear that the possible candidates are sensory, motor, and also conceptual process parts. The findings of the selective interference experiments coincide with the assumption that specific motor processes form the basis of retention following enactment, but they do not definitively prove that the enactment effect is based on motor processes. Here, too, it is desirable that experiments be carried out where individual process parts are systematically varied while the others are kept constant. One could be a variation of the motor similarity (cf. Chapter 5).

There are two positions concerning relational encoding. Bäckman and Nilsson (1984, 1985) assume that relational encoding is improved by enactment rather than by listening. Zimmer and Engelkamp (1989a) postulate that relational encoding is the same whether after listening or enactment. The multimodal memory theory has explained and analysed the assumptions behind this concept of relational encoding. In both cases it is a matter of categorical-relational information. This is restricted to the conceptual system and to the encoding of concept links that already existed before the experiment.

The findings on categorical-relational encoding are, however, inconsistent, as shown in Chapter 3. The findings of Zimmer and Engelkamp (1989a) correspond with the expectations of the multimodal theory, while the findings of Bäckman and Nilsson (1985; Bäckman et al., 1986) correspond with their expectations. Engelkamp (1990, chap. 5) pointed out that the findings of Bäckman et al. (1986) could be due to the specific conditions of their experiments and cannot, therefore, be generalised. These specific conditions could be the use of real objects in SPTs together with an organisation of the lists according to object category (such as toys, clothes, etc.) Further experiments must be carried out before a final evaluation can be made (cf. Chapter 5).

Over and above the evaluation of the findings on categorical-relational encoding, the multimodal theory leads to the prediction that the episodic-relational encoding of action phrases is made more difficult by performing the action than by merely listening to the phrases or seeing the actions being performed (cf. Chapter 5).

Effects of Automatic and Controlled Encoding

According to the multimodal memory theory, both automatic and controlled processes are able to set off conscious experiences when encoding. It is furthermore assumed that it is the extent of conscious experiences during encoding which is decisive for later recollection and not that these experiences are based on strategic processes. A further implication of these assumptions concerns expectations during experiments with double tasks. Secondary tasks requiring controlled processes lower recall performance for the main task by precisely the degree to which the latter contains controlled processes (cf. Heuer & Schmidtke, 1996). In other words, through secondary tasks requiring controlled processes, the conscious experiences during encoding of the main task which are based on controlled processes are reduced.

With these considerations in mind it is understandable that Bäckman et al. (1986) observed interference effects following enactment too, although they were significantly smaller than those observed following purely verbal learning. On the one hand, these effects could have occurred because encoding upon enactment is mainly, although not exclusively, carried out automatically, while with listening it is a controlled process. In this case we are dealing with central interference effects. The interference effects in the experiments of Bäckman et al. (1986) could, however, be partly structural and partly central. It is possible that the secondary task of counting backwards contains verbal parts that interfere with the verbal parts of the main tasks. In this case the common part of interference following listening and enactment would be structural and the additional effect following listening would be central. In order to distinguish the two explanations the task combinations would have to be varied with regard to the system components involved (Heuer, 1985; Navon & Gopher, 1979).

Besides explaining the findings of Bäckman et al. (1986), the assumptions put forward by the multimodal memory theory also explain the findings that Cohen made (1981, 1983; Cohen & Bean, 1983) and which motivated him to the assumption that encoding following enactment is nonstrategic. The fact that no elaboration or generation effects appeared following enactment is explained by the multimodal memory theory as follows: Upon enactment a rich, conscious encoding experience occurs automatically and can be improved little by additional controlled efforts. Since a rich, conscious encoding experience occurs automatically following enactment, a slower rate of presentation is of little effect either. Finally, the fact that controlled encoding processes following enactment are superfluous and a rich conscious experience occurs automatically accounts for the absence of effects due to age or intelligence. Such effects are mainly based on the fact that controlled processes improve with greater age and with higher intelligence. However, they are unnecessary following enactment.

In order to explain the fact that there is no primacy effect in the serial position curve for free recall after enactment it is necessary to consider the specific processes involved in recall. Before I go into a possible explanation of this lack of primacy effect following enactment I would like to bring the reader's attention to the fact that encoding following enactment, which appears to be optimal, in fact only leads to a recall performance of between about 50% and 80%. It seems to be inherent to free recall (particularly with unconnected items) that lists are not recalled in full, even if the lists are relatively short.

The explanations for the incomplete free recall are usually sought in the recalling processes. Rundus (1971) suggested that recalling the first items leads to the memory trace being improved and to the chances of recalling the items yet to be remembered being reduced. Similar considerations are to be found in Anderson, Bjork, and Bjork (1994). They, too, assume that recalling the first items inhibits the recall of later items (cf. also Bäuml, 1996; Tulving & Psotka, 1971). It may be postulated, furthermore, that incomplete recall should also arise due to the fact that the generation process in free recall does not usually ensue in accordance with a systematic plan.

The explanation for incomplete free recall and for the missing primacy effect in free recall following enactment given preference here also considers the causes to be found in the recall process. Recall is based on the items being generated. The generation is controlled via spreading activation through relational connections between items and is dependent on the items concretely generated and on their connections to other items. Since this process depends on a great number of coincidences, complete recall does not usually occur. This would require a systematic generation process. This explains why free recall remains so incomplete. If, in particular, the first items following listening were encoded systematically and under the control of metaknowledge, they could also be generated systematically in free recall. Then they would be recalled particularly well and better than later items. Corresponding systematic encoding processes for the first items do not occur following enactment, or at least not spontaneously. This is why no primacy effect is to be observed following enactment (cf. also Chapter 7).

The most important change in theory regarding automatic and controlled encoding processes relates to controlled processes. The distinction has been made between controlled processes as processes that are consciously employed by subjects and that occur in addition to the processes which "naturally" occur as part of the task—"listen to the phrase and perform the action described"—and between processes which bring certain aspects of the encoded information to the subject's consciousness. The latter contain both automatic *and* controlled processes. Retention should depend on whether information is made conscious upon encoding, and not on whether the encoding processes are employed voluntarily.

Most of the findings can thus be freely explained through the multimodal theory. In addition, the theory proposes more differentiated experiments in the areas where the findings cannot be explained definitively due to insufficient controls. Finally, the theory leads to further expectations, which can be tested in experiments.

CHAPTER FIVE

Empirical inconsistencies and theoretical controversies

In this chapter I shall investigate some important predictions of the multi-modal memory theory. Some of these predictions have been the subject of controversial discussion, not least because of inconsistent findings.

CONTROVERSIES CONCERNING MODALITY-SPECIFIC ASPECTS

The discussion concerning modality-specific aspects of the enactment effect is of major importance for the multimodal memory theory in a number of ways. This is because a distinction is made between modality-specific components and amodal conceptual components of the enactment effect to start with, and also because within the modality-specific components only the motor components are considered crucial for the enactment effect. No objections are made to the fact that perceiving objects improves the memory following enactment, but these effects are not considered crucial for the actual enactment effect. Planning and performing the action is considered relevant. Thus the sensory aspects of perceiving the action itself, for example upon visual perception of someone else performing the action or even upon enactment (at least without real objects), are considered to be different to the motor processes (planning and performing) in self-performed tasks and not crucial for the enactment effect. This clear division of sensory and motor processes and the assumption that only the motor processes are significant for the enactment effect are not completely shared by other authors (e.g.

Bäckman & Nilsson, 1984, 1985; Cohen, 1989a; Helstrup, 1987; Knopf, 1992, 1995; Kormi-Nouri, 1994).

The Role of the Object in the Enactment Effect

According to Bäckman et al. (1986), the use of real objects in performing an action is crucial for good encoding and for the enactment effect, since the object usually provides rich sensory information about its texture, weight, smell, temperature, etc. Motor information provided by movement in the action is just one of many aspects. According to the multimodal memory theory, however, planning and performing the actual movement are the most important factors of the enactment effect. Only these aspects are considered specific for the enactment condition. The sensory aspects tied up with perception of the object do promote retention but this is not specific to enactment, that is they improve retention following enactment no more than following hearing.

It has already been stated that the fact that the enactment effect is observable both when real objects are used (e.g. Bäckman & Nilsson, 1984, 1985), and when no objects are used (e.g. Engelkamp & Krumnacker, 1980; Helstrup, 1989b), refutes the position held by Bäckman and Nilsson. However, it must be stated that no direct comparison has been made between conditions with and without objects. Thus it remains unclear whether and to what degree the presence of objects influences the extent of the enactment effect. If the presence of real objects is crucial for the enactment effect then the effect should be greater when real objects are used. In a first approach Cohen, Peterson, and Mantini-Atkinson (1987) made a direct comparison between actions with real objects and actions involving no external objects, such as "nod your head". I call such actions "object-free" and refer in the other case to "object-related" actions. By Cohen, Peterson, and Mantini-Atkinson (1987), the actions were either performed by the subjects (SPTs) or by the experimenter (EPTs). Only in one out of three experiments did Cohen, Peterson, and Mantini-Atkinson (1987) observe an interaction between the learning condition (seeing vs. enactment) and the object condition (object-free vs. object-related). However, when there was a numerical difference between retention of object-free and object-related actions following enactment, the object-free actions were retained better. This finding was also reported by Norris and West (1991) and by Nyberg, Nilsson, and Bäckman (1991). These findings seem rather to refute a positive contribution of objects to the enactment effect.

The irrelevance of objects for the enactment effect had already been pointed out by Cohen (1981). He wrote (p. 269): "One feature of the tasks which did emerge during the course of the study, however, is that the level of

SPT recall was completely unaffected by whether or not the task required the cue of an object."

However, in all these experiments the status of the object was confused with the type of action (object-free vs. object-related). In other words, not only was an object used in one case and not in another, but also different actions were used in both cases. To my knowledge there are only three studies where the object status was varied while the item content was controlled.

Nyberg et al. (1991) compared free recall after SPTs with real objects with free recall after VTs, where real objects or non-real objects were presented. Their experiments show that phrases that are heard are retained better when real objects are presented, and that this improvement is so great that when objects are presented the enactment effect disappears. Unfortunately real objects were always used in SPTs, so that it remains unclear how far the introduction of real objects contributes to the enactment effect. A comparison where the presence of real objects was manipulated both for VTs and SPTs would be highly instructive in this respect, since using a real object when performing an action (e.g. "bend the wire") is obviously different to seeing a wire while hearing the phrase "bend the wire".

Such an experiment had already been carried out by Engelkamp and Zimmer (1983)—except that it was with EPTs and SPTs. In this investigation, the subjects learned identical lists of object-related action phrases. One group of subjects learned the phrases in EPTs without real objects, another group in EPTs with real objects. A third group learned the phrases in SPTs without real objects, and the last group in SPTs with real objects. The findings of this experiment are shown in Table 5.1. In this experiment two additive effects occurred. Real objects improved recall compared to imagining objects. Independently of this object effect, an enactment effect occurred.

Engelkamp and Zimmer (1997) have recently been able to replicate this effect several times. They varied the encoding condition (hearing vs. seeing

TABLE 5.1

Relative performance in free recall as a function of the encoding condition (seeing, enactment) and of the object status (real, imaginary) (Engelkamp & Zimmer, 1983)

	Encoding Condition	
Object Status	Enactment	Seeing
Real	0.53	0.39
Imaginary	0.45	0.30

vs. enactment) and object status (real vs. imagining) within a larger design using two lengths of list. The findings of these experiments are shown in Table 5.2.

In both experiments, there is an object effect and an enactment effect if EPTs and SPTs are compared, but no interaction of the encoding condition with the object status. These findings clearly confirm that carrying out an action is to be distinguished from perceiving an action and from perceiving the object of an action.

But the experiments also show that the object effect is larger in VTs than in EPTs and SPTs. The introduction of a real object improves retention while hearing more than while seeing or enacting, provided the list to be learned is short enough. This latter finding is in agreement with that of Nyberg et al. (1991).

To summarise, it may be stated that objects play no significant role in the highly efficient item-specific encoding processes of enactment. This becomes particularly obvious because the superiority of enactment compared to seeing does not change when real objects are introduced. However, the findings also show clearly that objects play a more important role in retention under the typical control condition, that is hearing, than with seeing or enactment. Perceiving real objects aids learning by hearing, which is normally a verbal form of learning, to such an extent that the advantage of enactment for retention can be reduced and in extreme cases even eliminated. This shows that when investigating the enactment effect a clear distinction must be made between factors that influence retention through enactment and factors that influence each of the conditions of comparison. The extent of the enactment effect can be influenced by both factors.

TABLE 5.2

Relative performance in free recall as a function of the encoding condition (hearing, seeing, enactment) and of the object status (real, imaginary) (Engelkamp & Zimmer, 1997)

Object Status	Encoding Condition		
	Hearing	Seeing	Enactment
Experiment 1 (18 items)			
Real	0.65	0.61	0.78
Imaginary	0.35	0.43	0.60
Experiment 2 (54 items)			
Real	0.36	0.42	0.63
Imaginary	0.13	0.27	0.46

Perceiving and Performing Actions

The findings reported previously (cf. Table 5.2) have already made it clear that there are two enactment effects. Retention after enactment is better than after hearing, but it is also better than after seeing the action. The retention superiority of enactment compared to seeing is clearly reported in the experiments by Engelkamp and Zimmer (1983, 1997), in further experiments carried out by Dick, Kean, and Sands (1989), Engelkamp and Krumnacker (1980), and Zimmer and Engelkamp (1984), and in a study carried out on 14-month-old children by Meltzoff (1988). Yet in a series of experiments Cohen (1981, 1983; Cohen & Bean, 1983; Cohen, Peterson, & Mantini-Atkinson, 1987) did not observe such an effect. Cohen's findings are summarised in Table 5.3.

These conflicting findings correspond to opposing theoretical positions. Cohen (e.g. 1989b) regards the encoding processes of seeing and of enactment as being largely similar and considers any differences to be negligible (p. 69): "Generally, EPTs appear to possess properties similar to those of SPTs, although in a slightly weaker form." The multimodal theory, on the other hand, emphasises the difference between seeing and enactment. It is only upon enactment that the motor system comes into play, that is that movements are planned and carried out (cf. also Meltzoff, 1988, 1990).

For this reason, Engelkamp and Zimmer (1997) made a special effort to find out the causes of the conflicting findings on the comparison between seeing and enactment. They assumed that the length of the lists might be the cause of the inconsistent findings. Cohen used short lists (12 to 20 items) in all his experiments, whereas the others used long lists (Engelkamp and Zimmer 48 items; Dick et al. 32 items). Engelkamp and Zimmer presumed that item-specific encoding only becomes better upon enactment than upon seeing if the lists are long enough, that is sufficiently difficult. It could be, for

TABLE 5.3

Average recall performance as a function of the encoding conditions of seeing and of enactment in various experiments carried out by Cohen

Author	Seeing	Enactment
Cohen (1981, Exp. 1)	56.5	53.1
Cohen (1983, Exp. 1)	48.0	47.0
Cohen & Bean (1983)		
normal subjects	69.1	64.8
mentally retarded subjects	55.5	59.0
Cohen, Peterson, & Mantini-Atkinson (1987)		
Exp. 1	51.0	56.0
Exp. 2	51.0	50.0
Exp. 3	51.0	66.0

example, that long lists require different retrieval strategies to short lists, for example perhaps the quality of the item-specific information is more significant in longer lists.

This assumption, however, proved to be incorrect, too—or at least in this generalised form. As shown by the findings in Table 5.2, the retention superiority of enactment compared to seeing in Engelkamp and Zimmer (1997) is, for the most part, independent of the length of the list (18 and 54 items).

These surprising, unexpected results gave Engelkamp and Zimmer reason to look for other possible differences between Cohen's and the other experiments. They found that Cohen had varied the encoding condition (EPTs vs. SPTs) between subjects, while Engelkamp and Zimmer (1997) had varied this factor within subjects. On the other hand, Engelkamp and Zimmer (1983) had also varied the encoding between subjects. This made it seem unlikely that this factor was a decisive one. None the less Engelkamp and Zimmer (1997) have replicated their experiments, varying the encoding between subjects. The results of their experiments for lists of 18 items are shown in Table 5.4. Cohen's findings were reproduced. No difference could be found between seeing and enactment.

Two aspects are remarkable. First, when one compares the recall performances achieved in the experiments in which the encoding conditions were varied both between subjects and within subjects it turns out that recall changes dependent on this variation following seeing, but not following enactment. Recall following enactment remains high in all cases. This could give reason to suspect that enactment produces a ceiling effect, were it not for the second remarkable aspect—the object-related items without real objects. Here recall was so low even following enactment (54%) that a ceiling effect can be ruled out.

The design appears to influence retention following seeing. If encoding during seeing and enactment is manipulated within subjects then actions that are seen are retained less well than if encoding is measured between

TABLE 5.4

Relative performance in free recall following seeing and enactment for lists of 18 items in length with different types of items (Engelkamp & Zimmer, 1997)

Types of Items	Encoding Condition	
	Seeing	Enactment
Object-free	0.68	0.69
Object-related, real	0.73	0.73
Object-related, imaginary	0.54	0.54

subjects. However, this conclusion does not take into consideration the fact that Engelkamp and Zimmer (1983) measured encoding between subjects and yet found that enactment gave an advantage over seeing. This led Engelkamp and Zimmer (1997) back to the assumption that the length of the lists were critical after all. They therefore replicated Engelkamp and Zimmer's (1983) experiment with a list of 48 items, but using different material. In this experiment they were able to reproduce Engelkamp and Zimmer's (1983) findings. There are obviously two factors that influence the retention superiority of enactment to seeing: the length of the list on the one hand and the experimental design used for the encoding factor.

One possible explanation for both factors of influence could be offered by the assumption that both factors influence the difficulty of the task. Short lists could be easier than long ones, and following one set of encoding instructions could be easier than having to alternate between two (variation within subjects). This assumption would explain the findings if the presupposition was made that learning by doing is simply more efficient than learning by seeing and that there must be a particular degree of difficulty to the task in order to make this difference in efficiency apparent. With easy tasks, retention is high under both encoding conditions. If the task becomes more difficult, recall performance after seeing falls behind.

Close examination of the findings, however, reveals that the length of the list and the design variation are not functionally equivalent. Although object-related phrases with imaginary objects were retained far less well than phrases with real objects, as shown in Table 5.4, yet even with imaginary objects there was not the slightest difference in retention between seeing and enactment. For this reason, the difficulty of the task is not a sufficient explanation.

A look at the literature reveals that there are at least two other retention effects that are dependent on the "between–within" variations: the generation effect (e.g. Slamecka & Katsaiti, 1987) and the bizarreness effect in imagery (e.g. Einstein & McDaniel, 1987). The generation effect refers to the fact that words that the subjects have to generate (e.g. in a word completion task) are retained better than words that the subjects only read. The bizarreness effect in imagery refers to the fact that bizarre sentences under imagery ("The stamp is stuck on the bicycle") are recalled better than normal phrases ("The book is on the table").

As regards the generation effect, a number of more recent investigations point to a trade-off explanation (Nairne, Riegler, & Serra, 1991; Serra & Nairne, 1993). The assumption is made that generating leads to good item-specific encoding while tending to impede good encoding of the item order. Reading, however, leads to good encoding of the order but weak item-specific encoding when encoding is varied between subjects. In agreement with this explanation, Serra and Nairne (1993) showed that the advantage in recalling the item order after reading items, observed in a "between" design, disappeared in a "within" design. It is presumed that in a "within" design good encoding of the order information under the reading condition is impeded by the fact that items are to be read and to be generated alternately, whereas good item-specific encoding after generating remains uninfluenced by the design variation. The multifactor theories of the generation effect also assume, in a more general form, that generating influences the degree to which item-specific and order information is encoded in comparison to reading. Einstein and McDaniel (1987) present similar ideas to explain the bizarreness effect in imagery.

Engelkamp and Zimmer (1997) made similar assumptions to explain the findings given earlier. They propose that seeing leads to poorer item-specific encoding and to better order encoding (more generally, to better episodic-relational encoding) than enactment, and that enactment leads to better item-specific and worse order encoding than seeing, and in a "between" design with short lists, this leads to a similar level of retention after EPTs and SPTs. When a "within" design is employed, then encoding and retrieval of order information is impeded by the alternating occurrence of seeing and enactment, and more so after EPTs than after SPTs. They further assume that good item-specific information may well be indispensable for the retrieval of long lists. They then apply these assumptions to explain the findings on the comparison between EPTs and SPTs as follows: Enactment may be observed to be superior to seeing if encoding of order is impeded. This is the case with short lists in a "within" design, because the alternate instructions of seeing and enactment makes this type of encoding more difficult compared to a "between" design. This explains the advantage of enactment with short lists in a "within" design. With long lists there must be an additional factor. It is not quite clear what this is. It could be that recall of long lists is always dependent on good item-specific information. In any case this is poorer after seeing than following enactment, regardless of the type of design used.

These considerations of the inconsistent findings on retention after EPTs and SPTs have led to a complex picture of the enactment effect. We had started off with the multimodal theory's assumption that seeing an action uses different subsystems than carrying out an action. According to our simple initial expectations, this should result in retention performances of differing quality. The idea behind it was that when comparing seeing and enactment, only differences in item-specific encoding should be relevant. The findings force us to assume that this idea was too simple. The involvement of both systems obviously influences not only item-specific encoding but also the encoding of episodic-relational information, and what is more, this influence is dependent on whether the two systems come into play in rapid alternation or separately. Finally, the dependence of the recall on the length of the lists presents a further complication. I will go into the repercussions of these complications for the multimodal theory in Chapter 7.

Planning Versus Carrying Out an Action

Together, planning and carrying out form the motor encoding, and together they bring about the excellent item-specific information following enactment. This hypothesis could be tested by investigating whether the "enactment" effect only occurs if actions really are carried out or if it also occurs when the actions are only planned or intended.

One problem that arises is the question of to how to realise the plan of an action without carrying out the action itself. If planning is tied up with the direct implementation of the action, that is takes place in the closest possible temporal proximity to the performance itself, then the attempt must be made to prevent the action being carried out—split seconds before, so to speak. If temporal proximity is not considered to be critical, then the intention to act can be regarded as the planning. In this case subjects could be asked to decide to carry out an action at a later point in time. If imagining carrying out an action is regarded as being equivalent to planning it, then actions that are imagined could be compared to actions that are carried out.

All three methods have been applied. I will give more detailed information on the comparison of imagined actions (i.e. imagined as self-performed) with the real performance of actions later in this Chapter (pp. 83–85). At this point I would just like to state the following: In free recall both with pair association learning (Engelkamp 1991a, 1995b) and with list learning (Ecker & Engelkamp, 1995; Knopf, 1992, Exp. 8) better performance was achieved following real enactment than following imagining self-performing actions. Furthermore, with list learning, free recall is better following imagining self-performing actions than after merely listening to phrases (Ecker & Engelkamp, 1995). If imagining an action is considered equivalent to planning an action, then these findings would seem to confirm that planning does improve retention of an action, even if not to the same extent as both planning and carrying it out.

Zimmer and Engelkamp (1984) tried to stop the process of carrying out an action directly before it was carried out. For this they tested three subjects simultaneously. One subject's task was to assess how well the actions had been carried out by the other two subjects. However, a concrete action was only ever carried out by one of these two subjects. When listening to the phrase, both prepared themselves to carry out the action, but only one of them was asked, randomly, to carry out the action. The results of this investigation showed that planning and carrying out led to better retention performance of the phrases (43.7%) than merely planning (26.6%). Similar findings were reported by Oesterreich and Köddig (1995, Exp. 3).

These findings also support the assumption that the full effect of carrying out an action really does require the action to be carried out and that merely planning it is not sufficient. As these experiments contained no verbal control conditions, however, it is still unclear whether planning improves retention at all in comparison to a verbal control condition.

The third method, to ask subjects to plan to carry out an action at a later point in time, has been applied in several studies. Such planning processes, however, are probably not identical to those which occur when an action is carried out directly.

Koriat et al. (1990) studied, for example, whether action phrases are recalled better when the subjects undertake to carry out the actions later (in the test) than when they learn them for later recall of the phrases. In this study planning led to better recall performance (0.63) than verbal learning (0.45).

From the parallel positive memory effects of carrying out actions (i.e. the enactment effect in many other studies) and planning actions in their study, Koriat et al. (1990, p. 577) conclude that "the two types of tasks share the same underlying representational code ... [and] that perhaps the encoding of future tasks entails an internal, symbolic enactment of the tasks, which enhances memory". They consider the nonverbal encoding processes involved in carrying out an action as the critical basis of the enactment effect, and they assume that the sensory-motor processes are triggered off just as much by planning an action as by actually carrying it out. In this case planning would be critical for the enactment effect and carrying out the action would be dispensable. In fact, however, they did not compare "planning" and "planning and carrying out".

A direct comparison of the planning condition as realised by Koriat et al. (1990) with the usual enactment condition and a verbal control condition was made by Brooks and Gardiner (1994). They also varied the length of the lists as an additional factor. They found better recall after enactment (0.51) than after planning (0.40). Retention after planning was no different to that in the verbal control condition (0.42). The authors express their surprise at the fact that they had not been able to replicate the planning effect found by Koriat et al. (1990), but could offer no explanation.

Engelkamp (1997) also compared a verbal condition with a planning condition and an enactment condition. In addition, a further condition was introduced in which the planning and the enactment conditions were combined. The motive for this condition is as follows: Basically, I consider the conditions of hearing, planning (hearing and planning) and enactment (hearing, planning, and carrying out) as increasingly complex conditions with regard to encoding. Further encoding processes are stimulated from one stage to the next. If the assumption concerning the increasing complexity of the encoding process is correct, then a combination of planning and enactment should be redundant. Additional repeated planning should not add any new information to enactment.

These four conditions were realised in the experiment as follows. The subjects heard 60 action phrases. Half of the phrases were only to be heard and the other half carried out. The words "Listen" and "Perform" were presented before each action phrase. It indicated whether the subject should only listen to the phrase (VT) or should also perform the action (SPT). One group was instructed to learn the phrases for a later verbal recall. The other group was instructed to learn the actions in order to carry them out later (motor recall). This resulted in the following design (Table 5.5). The labels given to the four experiment conditions are listed in the four cells of the table.

The results showed that the difference between hearing (0.22) and planning (0.27) was not significant. Enactment (0.44) leads to better retention than hearing and than planning. The combination of planning and enactment (0.37) was significantly less efficient than enactment alone. On the whole, these findings correspond to the results attained by Brooks and Gardiner (1994). The planning effect found by Koriat et al. (1990) could not be replicated here either.

I therefore carried out a second experiment, which only differed from Exp. 1 in that it was carried out as a group experiment and in that actual recall was therefore always verbal. This means that the retention test following instructions for planning (expected motor recall) did not meet the expectations of the subjects. The findings were practically identical to those in Exp. 1: There was no difference between retention performance following hearing and following planning; it was better after enactment and after planning and enactment than following hearing and planning; Enactment was better again than the combination of planning and enactment.

One possible reason for this surprising, unexpected absence of a planning effect seemed to be the experimental design used. Just as Brooks and Gardiner had done, I had measured the hearing vs. enactment encoding

TABLE 5.5
Design in Engelkamp's (1997) experiments

	Instruction for Verbal Recall		Instruction for Motor Recall (= Planning)
VT	"hearing"		"planning"
SPT	"enactment"		"enactment and planning"

Note: VT means verbal task, and SPT means subject-performed task.

conditions intra-individually. Koriat had not varied this condition. He had only compared hearing to planning and realised these conditions inter-individually. So I replicated the experiments with a pure between-subjects design (Exp. 3). Each group learned the action phrases under only one of the four conditions. Furthermore, I manipulated the factor of test congruency. Each subject learned two lists. The first list was tested congruent to the instructions (and expectations of the subjects). However, the second, which was learned under the same instructions as the first, was tested incongruent to the instructions. In other words, whenever a verbal recall was expected a motor recall ensued with this list, and vice versa. This factor had been added for two reasons: first, because Koriat et al. (1990) had found no test congruency effects, and second, because if no such effect were found here this would prove that the effects observed were the effects of encoding (and not of testing). If, for example, a planning effect occurred, it would also be proved that it is due to encoding processes.

The results of this experiment are summarised in Fig. 5.1. The test congruency did have an effect, but one that did not interact with the other four conditions. For this reason in the figure it was averaged across this factor. On the whole the recall performance with incongruent testing was somewhat poorer than with congruent testing. This may be due to proactive inhibition arising through learning the first list.

What is more important is that a clear planning effect is shown. Performance following hearing (0.34) is poorer than following planning (0.42), and these are both poorer than following enactment (0.50). Then

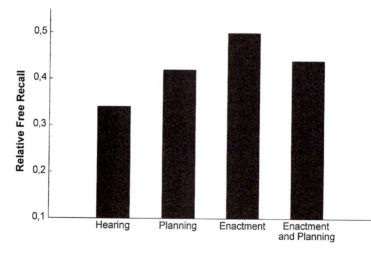

FIG. 5.1. Relative performance in free recall following hearing, planning, enactment, and enactment + planning (Engelkamp, 1997, Exp. 3).

again, the performance under the combined condition (0.44) is somewhat poorer than that following enactment. The positive planning effect was confirmed in a further experiment (Exp. 4), where only hearing and planning were compared in two independent groups (0.31 vs. 0.39).

How can this pattern of findings be explained? The results of Exps. 3 and 4 show that there is a positive planning effect (cf. also Koriat et al., 1990) and that this effect is weaker than the usual enactment effect, where enactment is added to planning. This pattern supports the theory that the enactment effect is a combination of a planning and an enactment component.

The absence of the planning effect where planning occurs within the context of enactment (Exps. 1 and 2) can be explained by interference between the planning components in both conditions (planning and enactment). The relatively poor retention performance in the combined condition can be explained by analogy. Here, too, planning and planning within the context of enactment could interfere with each other. As with the planning effect, both interference effects are encoding effects, because these effects are not influenced by the congruency of the test condition (cf. also Kormi-Nouri, Nyberg, & Nilsson, 1994; Norris & West, 1993; Ratner & Hill, 1991).

To summarise, the most important result is that the enactment effect is based both on planning processes and enactment processes. The enactment effect may be described as being a motor effect in particular insofar as the effect of carrying out an action is not exhausted in planning processes. It would be even more convincing if it were possible to show that even the types of movement involved in carrying out an action influence the retention of actions following enactment.

Motor Similarity

Since the multimodal memory theory assumes that planning and carrying out a movement influence retention of the action, it seemed obvious that we should vary the pattern of movement in the action and look for any effects of this variation of the movements. One idea which we thought of for an experiment was to vary the similarity of movement between old and new actions in a recognition test following hearing and enactment. This was due to the assumption that an effect on recognition memory should occur that depends on the motor similarity of the distractors to the old items. Distractors motorically similar to the old items should be more difficult to distinguish from the latter following enactment than hearing, because the movement components are supposed to form part of the memory trace following enactment but not following hearing. For the same reason, looking at it from the opposite angle, motorically dissimilar distractors should be easier to identify following enactment than following hearing.

These ideas were tested by Zimmer (1984) and later by Mohr et al. (1989). Mohr et al. (1989) varied the motor similarity between old and new items in two experiments. First, a list of action phrases was formed. In half of these phrases the object was substituted in such a way as to generate motorically similar distractors (e.g. "knead the wax" vs. "knead the dough"), and in the other half motorically dissimilar distractors (e.g. "pluck an apple" vs. "pluck a flower"). In the first case the movement patterns in the phrase pairs thus constructed were similar, and in the second case they were dissimilar. This means that the recognition list contained distractors that were motorically similar to old items, and distractors that were motorically dissimilar to old items. It was expected that the rate of false alarms for motorically dissimilar distractors would be lower following SPTs than following VTs, and that for motorically similar distractors compared to motorically dissimilar distractors it would increase more strongly following SPTs than following Vts. The results did not confirm these expectations.

There was no interaction between the type of encoding and the type of distractor. Motor similarity had no effect at all. The only effect to be observed was the lower rate of false alarms following SPTs compared to following VTs. Enactment makes it easier to differentiate between old and new items with both types of distractors than hearing.

There are two possible explanations for this pattern of findings. On the one hand, it is possible that the subjects base their decision in both cases—both with motorically similar and dissimilar distractors—on conceptual information. The attempt had been made to keep the distractors conceptually similar by substituting the object while retaining the verb (pluck an apple/a flower), but considering the relatively short list length the conceptual difference was obviously big enough to make a recognition decision on this basis alone. This argument is particularly critical for the enactment condition. On the other hand, under this condition the subjects had the additional possibility of differentiating between old and new items through the fact that they remembered whether they had carried out an action. This second mechanism is obviously only available following enactment and contributes to the overall superiority of the enactment group to the hearing group. Furthermore, the verbal presentation in the recognition test does not guarantee that the motor components of the distractors are activated and relevant for the decision. The situation would be different if the motor information were also activated in the test. We tackled both aspects in the following experiment.

The importance of a more thorough check of conceptual similarity is clear from an experiment by Cohen and Heath (1988). Due to the results of this study the authors conclude (p. 425) "that the different movement patterns involved in the various enacted events play little part in determining the recall probabilities of these items" and that "the actual movements associated with an enactment would appear to have little mnemonic importance". In short, Cohen and Heath (1988) vote against effects of similarity of movements. I consider their conclusion hasty. The title of Cohen and Heath's (1988) paper, "Recall probabilities for enacted instructions", is itself misleading, because in their experiments the subjects do not perform actions but watch the experimenter performing them. A more important aspect, however, is the fact that Cohen did not differentiate between motor similarity and conceptual similarity.

The multimodal memory theory assumes that the conceptual information determines the retention of items. It merely postulates that perceiving or carrying out an action improves retention, for various reasons. The critical point is that during enactment, motor information is encoded supplementarily to conceptual information. The motor information should, however, only become apparent if the conceptual differences are small. This is always the case in recognition, where discrimination between items is critical. We assume that as long as the conceptual information makes sufficient distinction between old and new items, the decision is made for the most part on the basis of this information. Sensory and/or motor information is only taken into consideration as well if new and old items are difficult to distinguish on the basis of their conceptual information alone. The sensory or motor differences between stimulus episodes are generally slight in relation to the differences in meaning and only become effective in recognition tests if conceptual discrimination is difficult. Discrimination is only difficult if the distractors are of conceptual and motor or sensory similarity to the original items, and then the false alarm rate should increase with sensory or motor similarity.

This has already been shown with regard to sensory similarity in experiments with picture stimuli, where the visual similarity was varied. With picture stimuli, too, the influence of visual similarity is slight as long as the distractors are conceptually different (Nelson, Metzler, & Reed, 1974). But if the distractors are conceptually similar (e.g. if a cup is to be recognised among other cups) then the rate of false alarms increases with increasing visual similarity of the distractors to the original (Bahrick & Boucher, 1968; Homa & Viera, 1988).

Since we assume that motor information is only activated if subjects carry out the actions when learning, we expect that—in analogy to picture recall—motorically similar distractors impede recognition following enactment, provided they are conceptually similar.

Engelkamp and Zimmer (1994a) therefore planned an experiment with orthogonal variation of motor and conceptual similarity between original and distractor items. They expected recognition following VTs to depend solely on conceptual similarity, while recognition following SPTs would also depend on motor similarity. The false alarm rate was expected to rise upon motor similarity, but only within the context of conceptual similarity. Discrimination performance (Pr = hits minus false alarms) after SPTs would correspondingly decrease in comparison with that after VTs. It turned out, however, that it was not possible to find enough items that were conceptually different yet motorically similar. They therefore only varied the motor similarity within the context of conceptual similarity, adding motorically and conceptually different items as a control condition.

They had the conceptual similarity of original and distractor judged in a pre-experiment. There were 32 pairs of phrases. These were either (1) conceptually and motorically similar (C + M +: wipe/clean the board), (2) conceptually similar but motorically different (C + M–: smoke/fill the pipe), or (3) conceptually and motorically different (C–M–: fold/tear up the paper). It turned out that the similarity of C + M + pairs was positioned much higher than that of the other pairs. The C + M– pairs, however, were also judged as being clearly more similar than the C–M– pairs. However, the result does not alter the prediction that the false alarms for conceptually and motorically similar distractors following SPTs should increase more strongly in relation to the other types of distractors than following VTs. These stimuli were used in two recognition experiments, which differed only in the criterion of answering upon recognition. All the subjects learned 3×32 action phrases, half of them by hearing and half through enactment. Half of the phrases learned by hearing and half of those learned through enactment appeared in the recognition list as old phrases. The other halves were distractors corresponding to the three categories listed previously. In other words, the subjects saw an item in the test either as "old" or as "a distractor". The results of both experiments render a uniform picture. They are summarised for Exp. 1 in Table 5.6.

Whenever the items are motorically different (C + M– and C–M–), discrimination performance is clearly better following enactment than

TABLE 5.6

Recognition performance following hearing and enactment as a function of distractor type in Exp. 1 (Engelkamp & Zimmer, 1994a)

	Distractor Type		
	C + M +	C + M–	C–M–
Hearing	0.14 (0.52)	0.57 (0.15)	0.59 (0.02)
Enactment	0.14 (0.81)	0.87 (0.10)	0.80 (0.05)

Note: C + M + means conceptually very similar and motorically similar, C + M– means conceptually similar and motorically dissimilar, and C–M– means conceptually and motorically dissimilar distractors. (Pr = hits minus false alarms) (Figures in brackets = false alarms)

following hearing. This difference disappears when the actions are very similar both motorically and conceptually (C + M +). Recognition performance following enactment is impeded by this motor similarity within the context of high conceptual similarity much more than following hearing. This effect is basically due to the fact that the C + M + distractors make the false alarm rate increase drastically following enactment. The experiments were based on the idea that motor information should influence retention following SPTs but not following VTs because hearing does not automatically lead to motor information being activated. As expected, the false alarm rate following VTs and SPTs was only different when the distractors were motorically similar, and it was only under this condition that recognition performance following enactment sank to the level of the hearing condition. This proves that patterns of movement contribute to the retention of actions following enactment. Carrying out actions makes it more difficult to differentiate distractors that are conceptually *and* motorically similar to the original than verbally learning the action phrases.

I pointed out earlier that a further cause of the false alarm rate being lower following enactment than hearing and of motor similarity not having made any difference in the study of Mohr et al. (1989) could be that there was no activation of motor information during testing. Following enactment the subjects were already able to decide whether an item was old or not on the basis of the criterion "I have/have not carried out the action". This information is not available to subjects following hearing. As the action phrases were not carried out upon recognition it may be assumed that the motor information of the distractors was not activated and therefore the motor similarity had no effect. Should these assumptions be correct, then carrying out actions in the learning phase would be crucial for recognition if they are also carried out in the test—in two ways.

First, if a phrase is repeated in identical form then carrying it out again should improve performance compared with a verbal recognition test. If carrying out an action leads to motor components being activated and stored, then the overlap of processes should lead to this information being used in a motor test but not necessarily in a verbal test.

Second, if a phrase that is conceptually and motorically similar is presented as a distractor in the test, then—due to the repetition of the motor components—carrying out such a distractor phrase should lead to the memory traces for this phrase being particularly similar to the representation activated in the test, that is more similar than the representation if the action is not carried out in the test. This should lead to conceptually and motorically similar distractors in a motor test being particularly difficult to distinguish from the originals after enactment. The false alarm rate should be higher in the motor test than in the verbal test. The rate of discrimination should be correspondingly lower. However, after VT learning we do not expect any changes in the number of false alarms or the recognition rate depending on whether the phrases are enacted in the test or not, since in this case no motor information was encoded.

We tested both expectations in experiments. First, I will report on experiments where we investigated whether, with respect to original items for distractors that are conceptually and motorically different following enactment, enactment in the test leads to better recognition performance than merely reading the phrases, whereas this variation has no effect following hearing.

In an initial experiment (Engelkamp, Zimmer, Mohr, & Sellen, 1994) the subjects learned 80 action phrases, half of them in VTs and half in SPTs. The action phrases were later presented in an old/new recognition test, mixed with distractors. The test consisted of two lists. In each list half of the items to be learned were tested. The first list was tested verbally. The subjects saw the phrases and assessed whether the phrase was old or new. The second list was tested motorically. The subjects enacted the actions for each phrase before making their old/new decision. As there were few false alarms in general and following learning by doing in particular, the discrimination scores (hits minus false alarms) were analysed. The findings are shown in Table 5.7.

Enactment during tests only improved recognition performance following learning by doing, and not following learning by hearing. This pattern was replicated in a further experiment. The findings reflect the fact that process overlapping upon enactment of actions both during learning and during tests is greater than upon enactment of actions during learning only, and the fact that the information which is made available by enactment in the test is not available following learning by hearing. This implies that through enactment motor information is encoded which can be made use of if it is also activated in the test through enactment (cf. also Fendrich, Healy, & Bourne, 1991; Perrig & Hofer, 1989).

If this is the case then motor similarity should also have an effect in tests following SPTs, provided the actions are also enacted in the test. This

TABLE 5.7
Recognition (Pr scores) as a function of encoding at study (hearing, enactment) and of encoding during test (verbal, motor) (Engelkamp et al., 1994, Exp. 1)

	Encoding During Test	
Encoding at Study	Verbal	Motor
Hearing	0.72	0.71
Enactment	0.84	0.93

assumption was first tested by Engelkamp et al. (1994) in Exp. 2. They manipulated motor similarity in the learning and testing phases by making the subjects carry out the actions either with the same hand or with different hands. Using the same hand should lead to more motor overlapping between learning and testing than using different hands. The conceptual information should remain unaffected by this manipulation. Recognition should be better using the same hand than by changing hands.

This expectation was confirmed by the results. Recognition performance was better when the same hand was used than when different hands were used. The results are listed in Table 5.8. During the learning phase phrases were also presented under a hearing condition. The results showed that recognition was in this case independent of the hand used in the test (right hand 0.69, left hand 0.63).

The theory that motor similarity influences recognition following enactment was investigated in this experiment by having the action carried out in the test using the hand either congruent or incongruent to that used in learning. As no action is carried out upon learning by hearing, a direct comparison of the effect of motor similarity following hearing and enactment was not possible. Engelkamp and Zimmer (1995) therefore varied the motor similarity in a further experiment which included the variable of material, as already done by Mohr et al. (1989) and Engelkamp and Zimmer (1994a). They had the subjects learn 80 action phrases. Then two distractors were allocated to each original. One was conceptually and motorically similar, the other conceptually and motorically different. Later, half of the items were tested with the motorically similar distractor and the other half with the motorically different distractor. In other words, each original item was tested with one of the distractor types. In addition to the similarity factor, the encoding was varied both while learning (hearing vs. enactment) and in the tests (hearing vs. enactment). The most important result expected was a three-way interaction of these factors with respect to the false alarm rate. The motor similarity should only have a negative effect following learning by doing, that is the false alarm rate should increase for motorically

TABLE 5.8
Recognition performance (hits) as a function of the
congruency of the hand used in learning and testing
(Engelkamp et al., 1994, Exp. 2)

	Hand Used in Test	
Hand Used in Learning	Left	Right
Left	0.88	0.82
Right	0.80	0.88

similar distractors if the action was also enacted in the test. The findings are summarised in Table 5.9.

As may be seen from Table 5.9, motor similarity only takes effect following motor learning and testing. Only after learning by doing are motorically similar distractors even more difficult to distinguish from the original items if they are also carried out in the test. As for the rest, the general increase in false alarms for the similar distractors is due to the conceptual similarity, which takes effect under all learning and testing conditions. It should be noted that no differential effects can be shown for the dissimilar distractors because recognition performance here was practically perfect.

It may therefore be concluded so far that the motor part of the information encoded through enactment is only visible in the recognition test if it is "forced" to be used in the test. This use may be extorted if the possibility of falling back on conceptual differences is excluded, that is if the distractors are made extremely similar conceptually to the originals. It may also be extorted by reactivating the motor information in the test through enactment. In this case it is used positively if identical items are repeated: An almost complete process overlap between encoding during learning and during testing is produced. The motor information has a negative effect, however, if motorically and conceptually similar distractors occur, because their similarity is increased by the reactivation of the motor information. The point that is less clear is whether conceptual information is better following enactment than hearing. If there is a conceptual encoding advantage through enactment, then according to the multimodal memory theory it should be restricted to conceptual item-specific information. It postulates no advantage for conceptual-relational information. The question as to whether this is supported by findings is discussed next.

TABLE 5.9

False alarm rate dependent on encoding while learning (hearing, enactment), in tests (hearing, enactment), and on distractor similarity (similar, dissimilar) (Engelkamp & Zimmer, 1995)

| | Encoding While Learning | | | |
| | Hearing, Encoding in Test | | Enactment, Encoding in Test | |
Distractor Similarity	Hearing	Enactment	Hearing	Enactment
Similar	0.20	0.18	0.19	0.26
Dissimilar	0.03	0.05	0.02	0.02

Summary

This section was concerned with proof of a multimodal concept of encoding processes. It was generally assumed that all possible stimulus aspects (visual, acoustic, smell, etc.) and aspects of carrying out actions (planning and enactment) promote retention. Moreover, a more specific aim was to show that what is particularly conducive to retention following enactment is the effects of planning and actual enactment. These assumptions are supported by the fact that presenting real objects, that is sensory stimulus aspects, improves retention (compared to a condition where non-real objects are presented), but that this positive effect occurs under all conditions and not just under the enactment condition. Put another way: The extent of the advantage of enactment compared to the mere perception of an action is independent of whether real objects are used or not. Only retention through merely hearing action phrases is particularly improved if real objects are shown in addition. This means that the control condition benefits more than the enactment condition from the introduction of real objects, and not vice versa. To get to the crux of the matter: Perceiving the objects is not the reason for the high level of retention following enactment.

As has been further shown, however, it is not perception of the action itself either. First, retention of self-performed tasks is independent of whether the actions are seen or not, and second, actions that are perceived but are carried out by others are retained less well than self-performed tasks (although only if the lists are long enough or if both conditions are realised intra-individually). Finally, it has already been shown in Chapter 3 that learning by doing suffers selective interference through carrying out other tasks. All of these results support the assumption that the high level of retention following enactment is not due to visual perception of the action.

However, this picture is made more complicated by the fact that retention performance for actions seen depends on whether they are learned in alternation with self-performed actions or whether only seen actions are learned. It would seem that the dependence of retention of actions seen has something to do with the encoding of order information and with the formation of new associations in the conceptual system. This aspect will be taken up again next.

If the high level of retention following the enactment of actions is dependent neither on the perception of objects nor on the perception of actions, then it is probable that it is dependent on the processes tied up with actually carrying out the action. This assumption is supported by the fact that it is not possible to reduce the enactment effect to a mere planning effect. It is true that retention after planning an action is better than after verbal learning, but it is still not as good as after carrying out the action. This supports the idea that the high level of retention following enactment is the combined effect of processes involved both in planning and in carrying out an action.

Here, too, the general picture is made more complicated by the fact that the pattern of findings described depends on the way the experiment is set up. It only occurs when planning and enactment are not realised intra-individually. In this case, retention following planning suffers if it takes place in alternation with enactment. In my opinion, this effect is basically due to the fact that carrying out an action includes planning it. This leads to structural interference effects which cause the weaker memory trace following planning to suffer in particular.

It would be proved even more convincingly that planning and enactment effects are enactment-specific effects if it could be shown that even the type of movement influences retention following enactment. The fact that this is the case was shown in two ways. First, it was demonstrated that action pairs that are similar both conceptually *and* motorically (i.e. their movement patterns) and of which one was learned and the other was used as a distractor in the recognition test were more difficult to distinguish than action pairs that were dissimilar. In these cases the similar distractors were often erroneously accepted. However, this false alarm rate was particularly high when the actions were learned through enactment.

The fact that movement information is significant for recognition following enactment was demonstrated in yet another way. It was shown that repetition of carrying out a movement in the test led to improved recognition of the action learned, when compared with the action phrase being merely presented. Actions that have been performed are better recognised if they are also performed in the test, rather than just the phrases being presented in the test. Finally, it was shown that this effect of repeating performance is reduced again if the movement in the test is performed differently to when it was learned (e.g. with the other hand).

CONTROVERSIES CONCERNING ITEM-SPECIFIC AND RELATIONAL ENCODING

The multimodal theory assumes that relational encoding takes place in the conceptual system (cf. Chapter 4). It distinguishes between establishing (1) new associations between concepts and (2) associations between concepts that already existed before the experiments. In the first instance I speak of episodic-relational information. In the second instance I refer to categorical-relational information. Episodic-relational encoding should be poorer through enactment than hearing, while there should be no difference in the use of categorical-relational information following enactment or hearing.

A special case of episodic-relational information is if actions are to be associated with the places where they happen to occur. This episodic-relational information is concerned, in more general terms, with forming associations between actions and action contexts, which have no inherent association with the action concerned. It should also be more difficult to create this association by carrying out the action. These three types of relational information are discussed next.

Categorical-relational Encoding Following Hearing and Enactment

As already described in detail in Chapter 3, in the study of Bäckman et al. (1986) subjects memorised categorically structured lists. The categories were defined via the objects used for the actions (toys, items of clothing, types of fruit, etc.). It was shown that organisation (indicated via the ARC score, cf. Chapter 3) and retention were both better following enactment than hearing. It was further shown that recall following hearing suffered more from counting backwards than following enactment. Both findings are to be expected, according to the theory of multimodally rich encoding.

As also mentioned earlier, Zimmer and Engelkamp (1989a) did not observe better relational encoding following enactment. They too had had structured lists memorised following hearing and enactment and had analysed the free recall and the ARC scores. Unlike Bäckman et al. (1986), they used lists organised according to typical action situations (working in the garden, preparing food, etc.), to taxonomic categories (such as cleaning something, touching something, eating something), or to movement patterns in the actions (e.g. making a fist, or using thumb and index finger like a pair of tweezers). Examples of items in the "make a fist" category are: squeezing a lemon, screwing up paper. The items were action verbs in Exp. 1 and action phrases in Exp. 3; Exp. 3 contained the movement categories. The lists consisted of six categories of four items each and eight categories of five items each. Table 5.10 shows the major findings in free recall and the corresponding ARC scores.

The data give a clear pattern. For lists which are organised according to action situations and taxonomic categories, the ARC scores indicate that this relational information is made use of, after both hearing and enactment. The information based on motor categories, however, is used neither following hearing nor enactment in free recall. Retention is always better following enactment. The consistent pattern is that there is no difference between ARC scores following hearing and enactment (cf. also Engelkamp, Zimmer, & Mohr, 1990).

The same pattern is reported by Zimmer (1991), after a slightly modified procedure. He also used lists which were structured according to categories, but there were differing category sizes. Larger categories were supposed to stimulate relational encoding more strongly than smaller ones (Hunt & Seta,

TABLE 5.10

Relative performance in free recall and mean ARC scores as a function of encoding (hearing, enactment) for lists drawn up according to action situations and taxonomic categories (Experiment 1) and to action situations and "motor" categories (Experiment 3) (Zimmer & Engelkamp, 1989a)

	Action Situations		Taxonomic Categories		"Motor" Categories	
	Free Recall	ARC	Free Recall	ARC	Free Recall	ARC
Lists in Experiment 1						
Hearing	0.48	0.52	0.36	0.31	–	–
Enactment	0.67	0.50	0.46	0.29	–	–
Lists in Experiment 3						
Hearing	0.31	0.22	–	–	0.23	–0.12
Enactment	0.45	0.21	–	–	0.45	0.10

1984; cf. also Engelkamp, Biegelmann, & McDaniel, 1998). This study produced two relevant findings. First, there was no interaction between the category size and the type of encoding (hearing vs. enactment) in the free recall test, as would have been expected if the category size had influenced relational encoding processes more strongly following enactment than following hearing. Second, there were no differences between the organisation scores following either hearing and enactment.

Engelkamp and Zimmer's findings therefore seem to prove that the enactment effect is not due to particularly good categorical-relational encoding but rather to good item-specific encoding. This assumption is also supported by the correlations between the free recall and ARC scores in Zimmer and Engelkamp (1989a). They observed a positive correlation between free recall and ARC following hearing in some cases, but no significant correlation was observed following enactment.

Altogether the findings coincide with the assumption that categorical-relational encoding processes on pre-experimental knowledge take place in the conceptual system. This knowledge is no different either for hearing or enactment. It consists of the information which also forms the basis of semantic priming effects (e.g. Lupker, 1988; Meyer & Schvaneveldt, 1971). The fact that retention is better following enactment is assumed to be due to the quality of the item-specific encoding.

I have already pointed out (Engelkamp, 1990) possible causes (different organisation principles and confounding encoding conditions with object status) for these contradictory findings in Bäckman et al. (1986) and Zimmer and Engelkamp (1989a). Engelkamp and Zimmer (1996) recently put these considerations to the test. They replicated the study carried out by

Bäckman et al. (1986), with one modification: They had the subjects learn the action phrases in the hearing and enactment conditions both with and without real objects. Their experiment thus contained the following three factors: type of encoding (hearing/enactment), type of object (imaginary/real), and type of interference task (no interference task/counting backwards).

The following effects were observed in the free recall test: More was retained following enactment (0.48) than following hearing (0.38). Retention with real objects (0.48) was better than without (0.38). Without interference (0.58), retention was better than with interference (0.28). However, there were absolutely no interactions. No differences were observed among the ARC scores. Moreover, the ARC scores were lower overall than both in Bäckman et al. (1986) and in Zimmer and Engelkamp (1989a).

The zero effects of the organisation were unexpected in two respects. According to Bäckman et al. (1986), higher ARC scores were to be expected following enactment than following hearing, and according to Engelkamp (1990) an interaction between the type of encoding and the type of object was to be expected. Neither of these expectations was confirmed.

As the retention performances did not replicate the findings of Bäckman et al. (1986) and as they also question their assumption concerning the automatic parts of encoding following enactment, Engelkamp and Zimmer (1996) carried out a further replication in which they stuck even more closely to the original conditions of Bäckman et al. (1986). The same main effects on free recall were observed as before, except that the object effect was no longer significant. What is more important, however, is that there was now an interaction between the type of encoding and interference. The interference effect was greater following hearing (0.42) than following enactment (0.33). This corresponds to the pattern of findings in Bäckman et al. (1986).

The ARC scores showed no systematic effects, however, although the scores now ranged similar to those in Bäckman et al. (1986). The mean ARC scores for the control conditions without interference in Exps. 1 and 2 in Engelkamp and Zimmer (1996) are reproduced in Table 5.11. But the

TABLE 5.11
Mean ARC scores under control conditions as a function of
the type of encoding and of the type of object in Exps. 1 and 2
in Engelkamp and Zimmer (1996)

| | Object (Experiment 1) | | Object (Experiment 2) | |
	Imaginary	Real	Imaginary	Real
Hearing	0.21	0.23	0.32	0.47
Enactment	0.19	0.31	0.44	0.44

findings of both experiments not only show that no differences are to be observed in relational encoding following hearing and enactment, they also show that the organisation scores are not influenced by the object type (real/ imaginary). This means that the confounding of encoding type and type of object status obviously did not distort the findings of Bäckman et al. (1986). This is also the case with the pattern of findings in the free recall test. Here the interaction of the encoding type and the type of interference, along with the lack of a three-way interaction that includes the object type, shows that the status of the object did not influence the pattern of findings in free recall in Bäckman et al. (1986) either.

The correlation between free recall and ARC in Experiment 2 proved to be significant ($r = 0.55$) following hearing. It was $r = 0.00$ following enactment.

These findings seem to prove that categorical-relational encoding does not explain the superior performance within enactment and that the effect in Bäckman et al. (1986) must be due to particularly specific conditions in their experiment, probably to special material properties.

Another carefully directed look through the literature for organisation effects following enactment produces the following picture: Bäckman and Nilsson (1984, 1985) observed more organisation according to the two item categories (object-free actions and object-related actions with real objects) after SPTs than after VTs, where no real objects were used. Subjects in their studies learned 8 lists of 12 items each and the ARC scores were based on the final free recall test, i.e. on $8 \times 12 = 72$ items, which fell into the two categories (object-free and object-related actions).

These findings of Bäckman and Nilsson's (1984, 1985) contrast with a number of experiments in which no differences in organisation were observed between SPTs and VTs. Norris and West (1993) only used object-free actions, which they divided into 4×4 categories corresponding to the parts of the body involved. They observed a low average ARC score (0.23) and no differences following SPTs and VTs. They further refer to Lichty, Kausler, and Martinez (1986), who found no encoding effects on the ARC scores either. Nor did Norris and West (1991) observe any systematic ARC effects for 16 items with and without objects, or Nyberg et al. (1991) for actions of which half were object-free and half were object-related, half of them learned by hearing and half through enactment.

It therefore seems that the positive organisation effects following enactment in Bäckman and Nilsson (1984, 1985) are basically due to three conditions: (1) to the dichotomous subdivision into object-free and object-related actions, (2) to the presentation of real objects in object-related actions in the enactment condition but not in the hearing condition, and (3) to the eight repetitions of the list structure. The combination of presentation of real objects and eight repetitions of the list structure in the enactment condition thus had the effect that the division of the items into two categories became conspicuous and effective.

Altogether it seems presumable that categorical concept knowledge which is already present before the experiments is not made better use of following enactment than following hearing and that in this respect the data support the assumption that categorical-relational encoding is restricted to the conceptual system.

Susceptibility to interference following VTs and SPTs is a different matter. Although in Exp. 1 Engelkamp and Zimmer (1996) were not able to replicate the interaction between encoding condition and interference in free recall observed by Bäckman et al. (1986), they were able to do so in Exp. 2. This interaction shows that free recall is hampered more strongly by counting backwards following VTs than following SPTs. This can be interpreted as being a case of central interference. Nevertheless, it still remains unclear why this is stronger following VTs than SPTs, although it may be maintained that this interference apparently affects item-specific encoding and not categorical-relational.

Episodic-relational Encoding of Unrelated Actions

Making use of existing connections between memory representations is not the same as forming new ones. The classical paradigm for investigating the formation of new associations is pair association, whereby unrelated pairs of stimuli are to be learned in such a way that at test the first stimulus is used as a cue to recall the second. The better the episodic-relational encoding of the item pairs, the better the performance in cued recall. It should be noted, however, that with pair association learning, not only does this pair-relational encoding take place within a pair, but also relational encoding between pairs (e.g. Hirschman & Bjork, 1988; McDaniel, Waddill, & Einstein, 1988). This chapter deals with the pair-relational information, which is the only one tapped in cued recall.

According to Bäckman and Nilsson (e.g. 1984, 1985), not only structured lists but also unrelated items should be subject to better relational encoding following SPTs than hearing (cf. also Helstrup, 1989b). According to the multimodal memory theory the opposite is to be expected (cf. also Engelkamp, 1986a, 1986b, 1991a, 1995b), that is that the association of unrelated actions should be more difficult in an enactment condition than in a hearing or even an imagining condition. The basic argument here is that the goal to perform an action restricts information processing to aspects that are relevant to that action. Enactment enforces concentration on the information relevant to the action. This causes any information not relevant to the action to be suppressed. Any actions performed are encoded relatively independently of each other, and this is an important cause of the high quality of item-specific encoding in the enactment condition. Looking at it from the opposite angle, it also means that it is more difficult to make connections and create associations between the individual actions than under other encoding conditions. These properties of performing actions stand in particular contrast to those of visual-imaginal encoding, of which it is known (e.g. Begg, 1983) that it is particularly suited to connecting items which are not yet linked in the conceptual system. In other words, visual-imaginal encoding has a positive influence on cued recall in pair association learning. This finding can be explained by assuming that visual-imaginal encoding restricts the processes of information processing less than performing the action does.

Thus there are two different positions with regard to relational encoding of unrelated actions following SPTs. The one assumes that the multimodal, sensomotorically rich encoding following SPTs promote relational encoding in general, that is including unrelated items. The other assumes that relational encoding of unrelated items is particularly poor after SPTs because performing an action focuses the information processing onto the individual items. There are contradictory findings with regard to this controversy too. I would like to show that this contradiction can be solved by looking at the findings in detail.

To start with, I will first report on findings on pair-association learning with nouns. For pairs of concrete nouns, it has often been shown that imagery instructions where subjects are asked to imagine the reference objects of nouns in interaction (e.g. a hat on a cat's head) lead to particularly good performances in cued recall (e.g. Begg, 1978, 1983; Bower, 1972). This has two aspects. First, it is shown that after interactive imagery instructions, performance is better in cued recall than in free recall. Second, performance in cued recall is better after instructions to imagine items interactively than after instructions to imagine the items separately.

These findings were originally attributed to the visual-imaginal coding system (e.g. Paivio, 1986). Bower (1970) reports, however, that instructions other than to imagine items interactively—such as instructions to make a sentence out of the two nouns in a pair—lead to completely analogous findings. Marschark and Hunt (1989) even explicitly rejected the assumption that the positive effects on cued recall of instructions involving interactive imagery are due to the visual-imaginal coding system and postulated instead that efficient pair-relational encoding is basically achievable with any other instruction involving integration of a pair (cf. also Marschark & Surian, 1989).

If the assumption that performing an action makes good item-specific information available but at the same time hinders the integration of unrelated actions is correct, then in an experiment on pair-association learning for unrelated action verbs free recall of the list items should be better after SPTs than hearing, as we already know, whereas cued recall should, in contrast, be poorer following SPTs than hearing. In any case the degree of retention superiority of enactment should be significantly lower in cued recall than in free recall. As the cued recall of concrete nouns following pair learning subsequent to "neutral" and in particular to integration instructions is better than free recall (CR > FR) but poorer than free recall when subsequent to item-specific instructions (CR < FR), as Marschark and Hunt (1989) showed, then it is also to be expected that, after enactment, cued recall is poorer than free recall. This pattern would even occur if explicit integration instructions are given, presuming that performing the action enforces item-specific processing of the items.

I tested these hypotheses (Engelkamp, 1986a, 1986b). In one experiment, the subjects learned 12 unrelated pairs of concrete nouns (such as hammer–church, sponge–umbrella) and 12 unrelated pairs of action verbs (such as break–put on, wring out–sharpen). The noun and verb pairs were to be learned in blocks according to standard instructions ("try to remember the pairs you hear") or according to modality-specific instructions. These consisted of instructions to imagine the items for the noun list and of instructions to perform the actions in the verb list. The lists were presented once, followed by a free recall test, then the presentation was repeated, followed by a cued recall test.

The findings replicated the better performance in cued recall as opposed to free recall for nouns. This shows that nouns are generally easy to integrate into pairs even if they were unrelated previous to the experiment. This effect was only slightly increased by instructions to imagine the items. Moreover, the findings showed that action verbs, on the other hand, were not so easy to integrate into pairs. This was especially the case if the actions were performed. In fact, after enactment cued recall was poorer than free recall. Finally, there is the usual finding that free recall was better after SPTs than hearing.

In order to ensure that the findings are based not on the different classes of word (nouns vs. verbs) but on the encoding modality, I presented the action verbs also under imagining instructions. Under these instructions, cued recall for verb pairs was better than free recall. That means action verbs, too, can be encoded pair-relationally, if it is imagined that someone performs the action.

To summarise, these experiments show that in principle action verbs, too, can be encoded pair-relationally, but that pair-relational encoding is impaired by performing the actions, while at the same time performing them promotes item-specific encoding.

This status of the findings was changed, however, when Helstrup (1989b), who replicated Engelkamp's (1986b) experiments in slightly modified form, reported findings that did not correspond to those of Engelkamp. Also,

Helstrup used 12 pairs of unrelated action verbs. He, too, used instructions to imagine and to perform the actions. In Helstrup's experiment, however, the cued recall test followed directly on the free recall test, that is without the presentation being repeated. Unlike Engelkamp, Helstrup observed two main effects. Cued recall was better than free recall, and the retention performances were better after performing the actions than after imagining them. Both effects were independent of each other.

I pointed out in a commentary on Helstrup's study (Engelkamp, 1989) that there are a few significant differences between Engelkamp (1986a, 1986b) and Helstrup (1989b) in the instructions, especially in the instructions to perform the actions. In Engelkamp (1986a, 1986b) the subjects were merely asked to learn the verb pairs by performing the action corresponding to each verb. Helstrup (1989b) altered these instructions in three ways. He asked his subjects (1) to think of a possible goal for each action, (2) at the same time to try to find a common goal for both actions in each pair, and (3) at the end to rate how well they had managed to find a common goal for both actions in each pair. On closer examination Helstrup (1989b) therefore, in fact, gave integration instructions. The findings could thus indicate that simple instructions to perform the actions merely prevent the subjects from spontaneously integrating the pairs, but that such integration is indeed possible after SPTs if the subjects are explicitly requested to do so.

Engelkamp, Mohr, and Zimmer (1991), therefore, carried out an experiment in which they used both Engelkamp's (1986a, 1986b) and Helstrup's (1989b) instruction conditions. They used 14 pairs of unrelated action verbs, which they had five groups of subjects learn under five different sets of instructions. They gave one group standard instructions (hearing) and the other groups different sets of instructions to perform the actions. There was a simple instruction to perform the action. A second set of instructions stipulated that in addition to performing the action the subjects think of a goal for each action, which could be achieved by performing the action (e.g. sweeping in order to get the room clean) (enactment, separate goals). In a further instruction condition the subjects were to perform both actions in a pair and then find a common goal for them (e.g. hammer and glue in order to repair something) (enactment, common goal). This condition was exactly the same as Helstrup's (1989b) enactment condition. In the last condition, subjects had additionally to rate their success in finding a common goal (enactment, rating). The subjects were informed that after the presentation of the list to be learned there would be a free recall test and directly after that a cued recall test. The results of this experiment are summarised in Table 5.12.

The findings reveal a clear pattern. The usual enactment effect was shown in free recall. More was recalled following SPTs than following VTs.

TABLE 5.12
Relative performance in free recall (FR) and in cued recall (CR)
for pairs of action verbs dependent on different encoding
instructions (after Engelkamp, Mohr, & Zimmer, 1991)

Instructions	FR	CR
Hearing	0.41	0.27
Enactment, simple	0.52	0.17
Enactment, separate goals	0.48	0.19
Enactment, common goal	0.50	0.33
Enactment, rating	0.50	0.33

Moreover, free recall following enactment proved to be independent of the variations in enactment instructions. These findings support the findings in Chapter 3, where it was seen that elaboration instructions and generation instructions have no effect under the enactment condition in free recall (Cohen, 1981; Helstrup, 1987; Nilsson & Cohen, 1988; Nilsson & Craik, 1990; Zimmer, 1984). The findings thus show again that the simple instruction to perform the actions in a learning episode already make the actions so easy to distinguish that it is difficult to improve the item-specific encoding any further.

The second significant result is that free recall was better than cued recall throughout and that the performances in cued recall varied depending on the instructions given. After enactment, cued recall was greatly reduced in comparison with free recall, as long as the subjects were not explicitly requested to integrate the verb pairs. Performance in cued recall SPTs was slightly improved, but not significantly so in comparison with merely hearing, if the subjects in the enactment condition were additionally explicitly requested to integrate the pairs. (It should be noted when comparing with Engelkamp's (1986b) findings that cued recall in that case was based on twofold presentation of the list and here only on single presentation.)

The findings of Engelkamp et al. (1991) indicate that enactment does indeed impede the integration of action pairs and that this negative effect on pair-relational encoding can only be compensated in part by explicit attempts at integration, though not completely. Unfortunately, these findings still do not concur with those of Helstrup (1989b), as Helstrup observed a clear superiority of cued recall to free recall whereas Engelkamp et al. (1991) did not.

For this reason a further difference between Engelkamp's and Helstrup's experiments was taken into consideration. While in Engelkamp's free recall all action verbs which were reproduced were considered, regardless of whether they were reproduced in pairs, Helstrup (1989b) only counted the reproduced pairs as being correct. It seems that free recall of a verb pair very probably implies pair-relational information, that is recalling one verb as an association with the other. This means that for the most part free recall is based on the same conditions as cued recall. Both performances should therefore be comparable. But when recalling pairs the subject has to remember the respective cue him- or herself, while in cued recall the cues are already given. Therefore, cued recall should be somewhat better than free recall of pairs. Engelkamp et al. (1991) then calculated the free recall for pairs, too. Table 5.13 shows the performances for this pair free recall in comparison with cued recall.

The findings show that performances in pair free recall and in cued recall were no different except under the standard condition, where cued recall produced better performance than pair free recall. The latter finding is probably due to the fact that generating cues in free recall is more difficult following VTs than SPTs. This is shown in the enactment effect for free recall of individual items. Hearing therefore benefits more, compared with pair free recall, from cues being given than enactment.

Although taking into account that pair free recall has reduced the difference between Helstrup's and Engelkamp's findings, the fact remains that Helstrup finds better performances in cued recall than in pair free recall while Engelkamp et al. (1991) do not find such a difference.

In my opinion the cause lies in the specific list properties in Helstrup's study (1989b). His verb pairs were probably less unrelated previous to the experiment than those of Engelkamp (1986a, 1986b; Engelkamp et al., 1991). This assumption is supported by more recent findings by Helstrup (1991). In these experiments the subjects learned 12 unrelated verb pairs under different instruction conditions similiar to those of Engelkamp et al. (1991). One result is of particular significance to the present discussion: in one condition in both experiments Helstrup asked his subjects to integrate the verb pairs during enactment. In neither experiment was there any difference in performance between pair free recall and cued recall (0.23 v. 0.21 in Exp. 1 and 0.21 v. 0.23 in Exp. 2).

TABLE 5.13
Relative performance in pair free recall (P-FR) and in cued recall (CR) for pairs of action verbs dependent on the different encoding instructions (Engelkamp, Mohr, & Zimmer, 1991)

Instructions	P-FR	CR
Hearing	0.17	0.27
Enactment, simple	0.15	0.17
Enactment, separate objectives	0.15	0.19
Enactment, common goal	0.28	0.33
Enactment, rating	0.29	0.33

These findings are very similar to those of Engelkamp et al. (1991). Overall, therefore, the data support the assumption that enactment not only impedes spontaneous encoding of pair-relational information but also makes the encoding difficult if the subjects are explicitly requested to integrate the pairs. Obviously, pair-relational encoding is inherently made difficult by carrying out the actions. I believe this is because of the necessity to concentrate on the action-relevant item-specific information in order to be sure the action is carried out smoothly.

To summarise, encoding actions by performing them has two inherent effects. First, carrying out an action makes available excellent item-specific information, and second, it prevents the actions being integrated into larger units.

Actions not only have the particular property that they can both be seen being performed by others and be self-performed. The same distinction can also be made with regard to imagining actions. It is possible both to imagine someone else performing an action—I call this "other imagery"—and to imagine performing an action oneself—which I call "self imagery". I have already pointed out that the processes involved in the visual perception of actions and in other imagery are similar and that in both cases there is not the restriction to action relevancy such as occurs when an action is performed. Both conditions should be relatively suitable for encoding pair-relationally.

A question arising here is whether analogue relations should be claimed between self-performance and self imagery of actions. Does self imagery make item-specific information available as efficiently as self-performance of actions, and is episodic-relational encoding impeded to the same extent? There is empirical evidence for the assumption that self-performing an action and self imagery are based on common processes (Heuer, 1985; Johnson, 1982). It therefore seems reasonable to assume that self imagery of actions leads to similar memory effects as performing them openly (cf. Foley, Bouffard, Raag, & Di Santo-Rose, 1991). Free recall for action verbs should be better under the self imagery condition than under other imagery, while the reverse pattern should be found for cued recall.

Engelkamp, Zimmer, and Denis (1989) compared free recall and cued recall for pairs of action verbs in pair association learning under other imagery and under self imagery conditions. Table 5.14 summarises the results. The data are significant in two respects: First, there is no visible difference between other imagery and self imagery in free recall; and second, cued recall is poorer following self imagery than following other imagery. The fact that the performances in cued recall are higher in Exp. 1 than in Exp. 2 and 3 is due to repetition of the list between the free recall test and the cued recall test in Exp. 1.

Completely analogous findings to those of Engelkamp et al. (1989) were observed by Denis, Engelkamp, and Mohr (1991). As they used the same

TABLE 5.14
Relative performance in free recall (FR) and cued recall (CR)
for pairs of action verbs dependent on the encoding
instructions (other imagery, self imagery) (Engelkamp,
Zimmer, & Denis, 1989)

Instructions	FR	CR
Experiment 1		
Other imagery	0.53	0.80
Self imagery	0.50	0.67
Experiments 2 and 3 (combined)		
Other imagery	0.46	0.46
Self imagery	0.49	0.37

material and followed exactly the same procedure as Engelkamp et al. (1991), their effects of self imagery can be compared directly with those of the self-performed actions of Engelkamp et al. (1991). Both findings are therefore shown together in Table 5.15.

The findings of Denis et al. (1991) correspond to those of Engelkamp et al. (1989). No difference was observed between other imagery and self imagery in free recall, whereas the cued recall was better following other imagery than self imagery. Moreover, comparison with the enactment condition shows that although there is no difference in cued recall between self imagery and overt enactment, free recall is better when the action is performed than when it is imagined.

To summarise, the findings on list learning and on pair-association learning show that for the excellent quality of item-specific encoding following enactment there must be additional causes to the necessary concentration on information relevant to the action. I assume that actually performing the action makes such additional item-specific information available and that this information is missing if one only imagines performing an action. On the other hand it looks as if both the internal and

TABLE 5.15
Relative performance in free recall (FR) and cued recall (CR)
for pairs of action verbs dependent on other imagery, self
imagery, and enactment

Instructions	FR	CR
Denis et al. (1991, Exp. 2)		
Other imagery	0.38	0.34
Self imagery	0.34	0.20
Engelkamp et al. (1991)		
Enactment	0.52	0.17

external self-performance of actions prevented episodic-relational encoding. This aspect of encoding is reflected in the poor performance in cued recall following both self imagery and enactment. Merely concentrating on the action does not guarantee high-quality item-specific encoding.

Episodic-relational Encoding of Actions and Places

In the method of loci, one imagines a familiar route, for example through the rooms of a familiar house, and associates with each room an item that is to be learned (Cornoldi & de Beni, 1986; Higbee, 1977). It seems that with visual-imaginal encoding, information already known about a place before the experiment is easy to associate with item information randomly given with it. The question is whether this method is equally efficient for motor encoding. According to the position represented here, it should be more difficult to create a new association between information on places and items through motor encoding, as enactment focuses information processing on carrying out the action and distracts it from the locational information. Under enactment conditions the subjects should spontaneously pay little attention to the locational information if it is irrelevant to the action.

Helstrup's experiments show that the loci method is of little efficacy following SPTs, even if its use is recommended to the subjects. Helstrup (1989a) presented his subjects with organised and random locations along with action phrases to be learned. The organised presentation of locations corresponds to the loci method as it is commonly used. The subjects go along a route they know and associate one action to each place. It is assumed that the knowledge of the route will be used later when recalling the items, through the subject reconstructing the route and recalling the actions belonging to each place. Helstrup left it to the subjects to decide whether they used this retrieval strategy. They were only asked to recall the actions. They did not have to recall the locations. In order to be able to estimate the use of the loci strategy, Helstrup also had a control condition where he presented the locations in random succession. If the loci method is used then free recall should be better for the organised presentation than for the random one. In one condition the actions were imagined, and in a second they were performed. The results of Exp. 1 are summarised in Table 5.16. While organised presentation of locations promoted retention of the actions compared to random presentation in the imagery condition, this was not the case in the enactment condition. Helstrup replicated these findings in two further experiments.

Cornoldi, Corti, and Helstrup (1994) also investigated the question of integration of actions with arbitrary locations in the usual pair-association paradigm. In these experiments the subjects were presented location names and action phrases. Either the subjects were to perform the actions (enact-

TABLE 5.16
Relative performance in free recall as a function of the
encoding conditions (imagery, enactment) following
organised and random presentation of locations (Helstrup,
1989a, Exp. 1)

| | Presentation of Locations | |
	Organised	Random
Imagery	0.64	0.55
Enactment	0.54	0.52

ment group) or else they were to imagine the actions (imagery group). They were informed that they would later be asked to recall the action phrases. Half of the subjects subsequently underwent a free recall test on the phrases and the other half a cued recall test with the location names given as cues.

The findings again confirm that it is difficult to integrate performed actions and locations. This is shown in two ways: First, cued recall following SPTs is poorer than free recall, and second, cued recall following SPTs is poorer than following imagery, although in free recall there is no difference.

In a further experiment, Cornoldi et al. (1994) tested the limits for the findings on the enactment condition by asking the subjects at study to give a reason why the action was to be performed at precisely that location. Under this condition better performance was achieved in cued recall than in free recall even following SPTs. These findings show that if the efforts are explicit enough an association can be created between locational and action information even under enactment. It should be noted, however, that in this experiment after presentation of the actions for 10 seconds the subjects had further 7 seconds to give their reason for the location–action combination. Hardly anyone would doubt that after carrying out an action it is possible to think about the action and about its relation to particular locations and that it is also possible to remember such thoughts if there is sufficiently time to do so. The multimodal memory theory does not exclude such possibilities. It merely attempts to specify the processes which are connected directly and inherently with carrying out actions (cf. also Zimmer, 1994, 1995a).

An investigation by Koriat, Ben-Zur, and Druch (1991) suggests that it is more difficult to integrate actions and locations under the enactment condition than under the seeing condition. They had pairs of subjects learn two lists of 24 action phrases in such a way that alternately one person carried out the action while the other watched him or her doing it. Half of the subjects learned both lists in one room, whereas the other half changed rooms between the two lists. Later all the subjects received the 48 old phrases together with another 24 new phrases in a recognition test. They had to decide whether each of the phrases was from the first list, from the second, or whether it was "new". Disregarding correct assignment to the two learning lists, the actions that were carried out were recognised better than those that were observed (98% vs. 94%). But if the number of phrases that were not only correctly recognised as being "old" but also correctly assigned to the two lists (i.e. the room the lists were learned in) are counted, then it was shown that practically all the actions that had been observed were assigned to the correct lists (i.e. rooms), as opposed to only 86% of the actions that had been carried out. This means it is more difficult to recall a place where one has carried out an action than a place where one has seen an action.

To summarise, locations that are arbitrary to actions are not encoded as components of the actions during enactment. Carrying out an action focuses information processing on the action itself and disregards the context that does not belong to the action.

Summary

According to the multimodal memory theory, relational encoding takes place in the conceptual system. Two cases are distinguished here: categorical-relational encoding of concept associations, which already existed before the experiment, and episodic-relational encoding of new associations between concepts in the course of the experiment.

Categorical-relational encoding should be no different whether action phrases are heard or enacted. Categorically structured lists therefore lead to comparable organisation processes in free recall following VTs and enactment.

The assumption that new associations between action concepts are more difficult to create during enactment than hearing and especially under imagery was also confirmed. In pair-associate learning of unrelated action pairs it was shown that cued recall was poorer after SPTs than following VTs and especially imagery. This contrasts with improved performance in free recall after SPTs than following VTs or imagining. Moreover, it was observed that following SPTs cued recall was poorer than free recall, while after imagining, equally good or even better performances were observed in cued recall compared to free recall. Although performance in cued recall following SPTs can be improved if the explicit request is made to integrate both actions, yet even then cued recall still remained below free recall. This indicates inherent problems in forming episodic-relational information in the enactment condition.

A comparison using unrelated pairs of actions that are learned by imagining the actions being carried out either by oneself or by others showed that (1) there was no difference between the two in free recall; (2) the free recall performances were none the less poorer in both cases than under the enactment condition; (3) there was no difference between enactment and self imagery in cued recall; and (4) the cued recall performances were poorer under these two conditions than following other imagery. This pattern of findings shows that episodic-relational encoding is difficult both under enactment and self imagery, whereas item-specific encoding is different in each case. It seems that the good memory trace for an action depends on the action actually having been carried out. This is what seems to raise item-specific encoding to a level typical of enactment.

The difficulty of forming new associations between concepts is also shown whenever locational information that has no pre-experimental connection with the action is to be associated with the actions. Here it was shown that recalling actions after carrying them out was not improved by an arbitrary location being added to the action. This contrasts with the supportive effect of such information under verbal and visual-imaginal encoding conditions. Locational information that is irrelevant to the action is apparently ignored during the encoding of actions carried out.

CONTROVERSIES ON AUTOMATIC AND CONTROLLED ENCODING

As to the question as to whether encoding during enactment of actions occurs automatically or in a controlled manner, there are basically two different positions (cf. Chapter 3): Cohen's (1983, 1985) position on strategy-free encoding and Bäckman and Nilsson's (1984, 1985) dual conception of both automatic and controlled encoding.

In Chapter 4 I added a further position to these. I share the assumption of the dual conception that both automatic and controlled encoding processes occur during enactment. Moreover, however, I assume that during enactment a rich awareness of the learning episode develops involuntarily and that this is why retention can hardly be improved. As retention is supposed to depend on the degree of awareness during encoding, it is automatically very good following SPTs.

Before showing that this additional assumption is necessary in order to explain the present findings, I would first like to recapitulate what led Cohen to assume strategy-free encoding through enactment and describe what led Bäckman, Nilsson, and their colleagues to first support and then give up the dual conception.

Cohen (1983, 1985) took up relatively early the position that encoding through enactment does not occur strategically. This position is mainly based on the following findings, which contrast with findings on verbal learning: After enactment there is no primacy effect in the serial position curve for free recall (e.g. Cohen, 1981); there is no effect of presentation rate

(Cohen, 1985); there is no effect caused by any importance ascribed to the various items in a list (Cohen, 1983); there is no elaboration effect (Cohen, 1981); or generation effect (Nilsson & Cohen, 1988). All these effects occur in verbal learning and are ascribed to strategic processes.

At first this position was also supported by the fact that Cohen and Stewart (1982) observed no age effects and Cohen and Bean (1983) no intelligence effects in children following SPTs, and that Bäckman (1985) and Bäckman and Nilsson (1984, 1985) observed no age-dependent differences in performance for young or old adults following SPTs. However, even after enactment, young adults retained more than old adults in later studies (Brooks & Gardiner, 1994; Knopf, 1991; Knopf & Neidhardt, 1989; Lichty et al. 1988; Norris & West, 1991). Similarly, Kausler and his colleagues reported age effects in a slightly modified paradigm (Kausler, 1989, 1994; Kausler, Lichty, & Freund, 1985; Kausler et al. 1986).

Cohen, Sandler, and Schroeder (1987) were able to isolate list length as a factor which probably contributes to the inconsistent findings. Age differences arose after enactment for long lists, but not for short ones. Although list length could well be a crucial variable in this context, it is not sufficient as an explanation, since Kausler (e.g. 1989) and also Knopf (1991, 1992) observed age effects following SPTs for short lists too. None the less, very short lists can be so easy that after enactment even the "weaker" older learners obtain good results, which are no different to those of younger learners.

Bäckman and Nilsson (1984, 1985, cf. Chapter 3) assume that verbal encoding includes controlled processes while nonverbal encoding ensues automatically. They regard learning through enactment as a mixed task, which contains both verbal and nonverbal components. And, in their opinion, it is because learning by doing also contains nonverbal components that older people still achieve relatively good results too. This position is also supported by the fact that retention following both enactment and hearing is impaired by supplementary tasks which demand attention (such as counting backwards) but more so following learning by hearing than learning by doing (cf. Chapter 3).

Bäckman and Nilsson and their colleagues have investigated this "dual encoding" conception in more detail in a series of experiments. The basic idea was to test the verbal encoding components via recall of the verbs and objects in action phrases and the nonverbal encoding components via recall of nonverbal aspects such as texture, weight, and colour of the objects of the actions. In order to do this, Bäckman, Nilsson, Herlitz, Nyberg, and Stigsdotter (1991) checked retention of the action verbs in free recall and retention of the object properties (colour and weight) in cued recall (the object names served as cues) both with disturbance through an additional task and without disturbance. The interference task consisted of counting backwards. The subjects were explicitly requested to learn the verbs and the object properties. As expected, the interference task impeded retention performance for the colours and weights of the objects less than retention of the verbs. Since retention of verbs was tested in free recall and that of the object properties in cued recall in this study, they carried out further investigations where they tested both components using the same procedure.

In Exp. 1, Bäckman, Nilsson, and Kormi-Nouri (1993) tested retention of verbs and of the colours of the objects in the actions in cued recall, using the object names as cues in both cases. In a second experiment they compared retention of the objects and their colours by using the verbs as cues. In both experiments it was observed that the interference task impeded retention of the verbal components more strongly (0.70 v. 0.41 in Exp. 1 and 0.49 v. 0.35 in Exp. 2) than retention of the nonverbal components (0.61 v. 0.43 in Exp. 1 and 0.28 v. 0.24 in Exp. 2).

In the authors' opinion both investigations show that the verbal components (verb and object recall) were affected more by the interference task than the nonverbal components (object colour).

It cannot be excluded that counting backwards has a different interference effect on the verbal and nonverbal encoding processes, because counting backwards contains a verbal component. For this reason, Kormi-Nouri, Nilsson, and Bäckman (1994) introduced a new, nonverbal interference task with verbal components. The subjects now saw coloured dots of two colours (red and black) during the learning phase. The encoding of these dots represents the nonverbal part of the task. The number of coloured dots varied from one presentation to another. The red dots had to be counted and added up in the course of the presentations. This corresponded to the verbal encoding components. All other conditions were identical to those of Bäckman et al. (1993). The results of this study are summarised in Table 5.17.

The authors interpret the findings that there was no interaction in either experiment as an indication that the position on dual encoding during enactment is not tenable and "that encoding of verbal and physical components of SPTs may not differ with respect to attentional demands. That is, SPTs are entirely attention-demanding and effortful" (Kormi-Nouri et al., 1994, p. 45).

The conclusion that learning during enactment is "entirely" demanding on attention, that is to the same extent as learning action phrases verbally, seems to me not to be justified by the given data. This conclusion is based, for example, on the assumption that the verbal and nonverbal components of the interference task interfere with the corresponding structural components of the learning task to an equal degree. This could, coincidentally, be the case, but it could equally well not be the case. A further obstacle to clear interpretation is presented by the fact that there are differences in retention

TABLE 5.17
Relative cued recall following SPTs without interference and with
interference (a) for verbs and object colours with object names as cues in
Exp. 1 and (b) for objects and object colours with action verbs as cues in
Exp. 2 (Kormi-Nouri, Nilsson, & Bäckman, 1994)

	(a) Object Name as Cue (Exp. 1)	
	Cued Verb Recall	Cued Colour Recall
Without interference	0.85	0.73
With interference	0.76	0.58

	(b) Verb as Cue (Exp. 2)	
	Cued Object Recall	Cued Colour Recall
Without interference	0.66	0.36
With interference	0.56	0.24

performance even under the control conditions. I also consider the chosen procedure to be a problem in that colour recall always presupposes object recall (since the colour of a certain object has to be recalled). Object recall, however, is regarded by the authors as being an indicator for verbal encoding. Another point of argument is whether colour is not verbally encoded information too.

Despite these problems I consider the assumption of dual encoding interesting and also the assumption that verbal and enactment learning require controlled processes to differing degrees. Considering the experiments carried out by Bäckman, Nilsson, and their colleagues, it seems to me that the best justified conclusion is that encoding during enactment also contains controlled components. In this respect it is not tenable strictly to assume strategy-free encoding through enactment, in spite of the phenomena presented by Cohen (e.g. 1989a). On the other hand, the strict assumption that encoding during enactment is controlled cannot ignore Cohen's (1985) findings to support his position. As an explanation for Cohen's findings I have formulated the additional assumption that enactment automatically leads to excellent item-specific encoding, that is to consciously experiencing the individual episodes to such a degree that it ensures a high level of retention following SPTs. In this context it is interesting that Cohen himself (1989a) allows for different kinds of possible controlled processes during encoding through enactment and distinguishes them from their potential effectiveness for retention.

CHAPTER SIX

Theoretical integration II: Expansion and differentiation of the multimodal theory

EFFECTS OF MULTIMODAL ENCODING

Over the past few years Hubert Zimmer and I have carried out a systematic investigation of the question of whether perceiving the actions themselves and perceiving the objects used in the actions influence retention independently of each other and also of carrying out the action. The results of these studies show that perceiving the objects of actions, perceiving the bodily movements of someone else performing the action, and performing the action oneself influence retention independently of each other. Therefore, perceiving the object of an action, perceiving another person's performance, and perceiving one's own performance of an action must all be considered as different determinants of memory performance (cf. also Meltzoff, 1988, 1990). It also means that the size of the enactment effect is independent of perception of the objects of the actions. Furthermore, it became clear that visual perception of self-performance is not critical for the enactment effect either; it occurs even if actions are performed with the eyes closed.

The system which encodes the fact that a particular object is involved in an action works independently of the system which, on the basis of visual perception, encodes the fact that a particular action is performed, and this system in turn works independently of the system which encodes our own movements when carrying out an action.

Comparison of retention performance for actions seen and self-performed has also, however, led to unexpected results. The retention superiority of enactment to seeing, for example, only appeared when both encoding conditions were realised as a within-subjects factor or when the list to be memorised was very long. This complication of the findings was explained through the assumption that seeing actions leads to poorer item-specific encoding processes but also to better episodic-relational encoding processes than carrying out actions, and that a within-subjects variation of the encoding conditions impedes episodic-relational encoding, which the seeing condition would suffer under in particular. These assumptions extend the multimodal memory theory.

The first expansion relates to the assumption that poorer item-specific encoding and better episodic-relational encoding upon seeing actions and better item-specific encoding and poorer episodic-relational encoding upon performing actions balance each other out with regard to free recall, so long as the list to be memorised is not too long. The second expansion relates to the length of the list to be memorised. One explanation suggested is that the item-specific information is more important than the episodic-relational information when recalling long lists. The third expansion concerns the assumption that episodic-relational encoding of actions seen is impeded by the fact that it occurs in the context of actions performed. Introducing actions performed between actions seen apparently impedes the establishment of new associations between the actions seen by focusing on the information that is relevant to the actions during performance.

Closer examination of the processes involved in enactment led to the investigation of planning and enactment. The critical question in this context was whether the enactment effect can be reduced to planning processes. The investigations showed that planning does improve retention compared to the control condition, but that additionally enacting the planned action improved the retention performance further. It is assumed that the two activities—planning and enacting—ensue in different subsystems of the motor system. In this respect the findings on planning actions also correspond to the assumptions of the multimodal memory theory.

Yet an unexpected result was found here, too. It is again the experimental design which influences the results. Encoding of the planning alone is different from the encoding of planning of enactment. Encoding through enactment impedes the additional encoding of planning. I interpret this as interference of the overlapping planning processes. The planning involved in the normal enactment condition impedes this simultaneous planning aimed at later enactment.

But these differentiating considerations do not alter the assumption that carrying out actions leads to outstanding item-specific encoding and that the enactment itself plays an important role.

If not only planning but also carrying out an action influences retention then the question arises as to whether the pattern of movements is also stored and influences retention. It was shown that both re-enacting the tasks in the test and the similarity of movements in the tasks learned and in distractor tasks influence recognition memory. The similarity of movements only had an effect, however, if the conceptual meaning of the distractor was similar to that of the original. Altogether these findings show that not only the information that an action *was* performed, but also *how* it was performed is stored.

EFFECTS OF ITEM-SPECIFIC AND RELATIONAL ENCODING

Basically, one new finding has been made with regard to item-specific information: Planning or imagining self-performance of an action is not sufficient to make available the excellent item-specific information which becomes available through actual enactment. The results again emphasise the fact that sensory encoding processes are irrelevant for the enactment effect, which leaves conceptual and motor item-specific processes as the essential basis of the enactment effect.

A differentiation was made in relational information. Besides the associations already existing in the conceptual system between actions before experiments, that is categorical-relational information, episodic-relational information was postulated. This second type relates to the establishment of hitherto nonexistent associations between actions in the learning episode. It was postulated that not only does carrying out actions not promote the establishment of new episodic-relational associations (in the conceptual system) compared with hearing or imagining them, but even makes it more difficult.

It was assumed that carrying out actions forces focusing onto the information relevant to the actions in such a way that the planning of the action is screened off from other information. This is the only way to ensure that the action is carried out without interference (cf. Neumann, 1992). Such focusing on information relevant to the action is not forced into play through other modalities (such as seeing actions or imagining their performance by others). There is no problem if, when watching apples being picked, we widen our range of vision and include the context. But if we want to pick an apple ourselves it can easily happen that we miss the apple if we do not concentrate our attention on picking it. Thus, carrying out an action promotes item-specific encoding while impeding its episodic-relational encoding. There should be no problem, however, in using existing categorical-relational associations in enactment, since these are activated and made available for use automatically. This use of categorical-relational information should be no better upon enactment than with other encoding modalities, which basically activate the same concepts and their associations.

These assumptions are supported by the findings. Pre-experimental categorical associations between actions are used to the same extent under hearing and enactment conditions. Yet the enactment effect remains. This, too, suggests that it is due to good item-specific encoding. This in turn impedes the establishment of new associations between actions, as shown by the results of the cued recall tests in the pair-association paradigm with unrelated actions. When unrelated actions were memorised it was found constantly that free recall of verbs after enactment was better than cued recall. The opposite effect was shown after imagining external performance of actions. Accordingly, the usual enactment effect was observed upon free recall, whereas an inverted enactment effect occurred upon cued recall. Even after explicit requests to integrate the action pairs under enactment conditions, performance continued to be lower in cued recall than in free recall.

Differentiations are also necessary in the assumptions concerning the encoding of the episodic-relational encoding of actions. On the one hand, imagining performing a task oneself leads to a focusing on the information relevant to the action in a way similar to actually performing the task. This was shown in the cued recall performance, which was equally poor under both conditions and poorer in both cases than after imagining someone else performing the tasks. On the other hand, the high performance in free recall that occurs after enactment does not occur after imagining self-performance of the tasks. This shows once again that actually carrying out an action is important for the enactment effect. Imagining self-performance of a task is just as inadequate for the effect as merely planning it. Only the command to perform a task gives the memory trace the high distinctiveness that the enactment effect is based on.

The assumption that self-performance of a task promotes the processing of the information relevant to that action and thus impedes association with other actions that happen to take place in its temporal vicinity can be generalised to other context information which happens to be present. This, too, is difficult to associate with the actions in enactment conditions, because enactment focuses processing onto the information relevant to the action. The place in which an action happens to take place is irrelevant, for instance.

EFFECTS OF AUTOMATIC AND CONTROLLED ENCODING

In the case of performance of an action upon presentation of an action phrase I assume that enactment is always initiated by an act of will. This leads to the conclusion that learning through the enactment of tasks always includes controlled processes, too.

If the encoding of actions following hearing and enactment is compared, then with hearing there is no act of will such as is tied up with enactment. Also, the instruction to listen to the action phrases gives the subjects a less clear objective. However, this unspecific instruction to listen linked with the objective of retaining the items permits active processing processes. The subjects can deploy active processing strategies as they see fit in order to improve their retention of the phrases. That means that although hearing itself requires no more controlled processes than enactment (less, in fact), more controlled processes are usually deployed due to the intention to retain the items. These processes, which are employed strategically and which complement "mere" hearing and understanding, improve retention following hearing and are very easily disrupted by secondary tasks that also require controlled processes. But the narrow objective under the enactment condition not only leads to the voluntary, that is controlled performance of actions, it also leads to a rich conscious experience being produced with every action. This high degree of awareness during encoding is an automatic consequence of performing actions and the reason why they are recalled well. These assumptions tie in with the fact that retention performance is more strongly disrupted following hearing than following enactment by secondary tasks that also require controlled processes. Yet they disrupt retention after enactment, too.

These considerations also tie in with the observations Cohen (e.g. 1983, 1985) regarded as indicative of strategy-free encoding after enactment (no primacy effect, no effect of presentation rate, no age effect, and no elaboration effect).

In my opinion, these observations are due to two characteristics of encoding after enactment. First, carrying out an action prevents spontaneous encoding processes that extend beyond those directly connected with the enactment, such as the active search for associations with other conceptual information, and those processes known as rehearsal processes. Second, even if such active processes are explicitly triggered (e.g. through appropriate additional instructions) they do not normally influence retention after enactment, because the encoding processes occurring spontaneously already create optimal conditions for recalling the different items.

After hearing it is a different matter. As with linguistic stimuli in general, hearing does not "automatically" lead to a rich consciousness of the items and to efficient memory traces. In order to create efficient memory traces with verbal stimuli, additional active elaboration processes in the conceptual system are needed. These additional processes take time and can be stimulated by appropriate instructions. Therefore retention after hearing depends on presentation time and instructions to elaborate.

These two aspects explain the phenomena Cohen observed as follows. Active processes are particularly beneficial to the first items in a list and lead to a primacy effect in the serial position curve. This effect does not occur after enactment because such processes do not occur spontaneously after enactment.

The fact that active additional processes are deployed after hearing but not after enactment also explains why the rate of presentation (at least within particular limits) has an effect on retention after hearing but not after enactment.

The fact that age and intelligence exert little influence on retention after enactment is due to the fact that our memories function well naturally with regard to self-performed actions. However, good functioning is limited, and it also declines with age. This becomes apparent when the lists to be memorised are longer or more difficult to memorise for some other reason. However, with the current state of findings it is difficult to find an answer to the question of whether impairment through age is less severe after enactment than after hearing, for instance, because performance is usually poorer after hearing than after enactment anyway, which means any further fall in performance already starts off from different levels. Either way, the assumption that with increasing age the self-initiated, active additional processes become more difficult and more seldom seems to be plausible and an important determinant of memory deterioration in old age (cf. Craik & Jennings, 1992).

Finally, the fact that retention after enactment can hardly be influenced by explicit instructions for additional encoding processes corresponds with the assumption that the encoding processes occurring spontaneously after enactment are already very efficient, for the reason given previously.

With their concept of dual encoding after enactment, Bäckman and Nilsson (1984, 1985; Bäckman et al., 1993) in particular held the position that encoding after enactment consisted of controlled verbal components on the one hand and automatic nonverbal components on the other. They recently relinquished this position (Kormi-Nouri, Nilsson, & Bäckman, 1994). They concluded that encoding through enactment was entirely attention-demanding. However, the relevant findings from the interference experiments reported in Chapter 5 are inconsistent and do not allow a clear conclusion.

The central conclusion which can be drawn in this context is that structural and central interference should be distinguished. There are central or controlled processes that disrupt each other because they use the common, limited resource of a central processor. There are also automatic processes that disrupt each other because they override each other. Structural interferences make memory traces more difficult to discriminate. Even if one does not share the resource argument for the controlled processes, still the plausible assumption remains that the controlled processes could disrupt each other in a different way, closely connected with processes of attention, while automatic processes could disrupt each other by masking each other. The latter, at least, corresponds to the system-specific interference we looked at in our early interference experiments (cf. Chapter 3). This interference was assumed to depend on the specific processes connected with the systems involved in encoding.

CHAPTER SEVEN

Recent studies on encoding and retrieval

Until recently, all the investigations on retention following enactment located the causes of the enactment effect in encoding. Recent investigations have been directing increasing attention to the processes involved during retrieval. This makes the situation more complicated, because retention is considered an interplay of the specific processes involved in encoding and in retrieval. Although this interplay appears repeatedly throughout Chapter 7, I shall start with some new aspects in encoding and continue with differentiations in the concept of retrieval processes before I explicitly deal with the interplay of encoding and retrieval.

RECENT FINDINGS ON ENCODING

The Internal Structure of Actions

Up to here the main focus of attention on the subject of "relational" encoding has been the relationship between actions. Now we focus on the encoding of individual actions. Since action phrases generally consist of an action verb and an object word, the elements of each individual phrase or action must be integrated into a single unit in the memory. It was Kormi-Nouri (1994) above all who shifted attention to the intra-item relational information. He considers two types of relationships which can exist between verbs and nouns, or between actions and objects—a pre-experimental semantic relationship and an episodic one. He assumes that both kinds of relationship are promoted through enactment rather than through hearing. According to Kormi-Nouri, the better episodical integration of action phrases after enactment than after hearing is assumed to be increased if there are also pre-experimental semantic relationships between the verb and the object. That is, the degree of semantic integration, which he varies via the material, and the degree of episodic integration, which he varies via the encoding conditions (hearing/enactment), should interact in recall. He therefore expects the enactment effect to be greater for well-integrated phrases than for poorly integrated phrases, that is if previous to the experiment there are hardly any associations between verb and object.

This hypothesis contrasts with the expectations arising from the multimodal memory theory, according to which the enactment effect is an effect of episodic integration. Pre-experimental semantic relationships between the verbs and object words of phrases are assumed to be situated in the conceptual system, and to have similar effects after both hearing and enactment. Semantic and episodic integration would therefore be expected to have independent effects. Semantic relationships within phrases would be no different in their effects on encoding whether after enactment or hearing, since the effect is due to processes of automatic activation spread between the concepts involved. Episodic integration within phrases is expected to be more successful after enactment than after hearing, because enactment focuses the processing processes onto the information relevant to the action and so promotes action–object integration.

According to the multimodal theory, semantic and episodic integration of phrases can be examined most directly in a cued recall test, where the object serves as a cue for the verb or vice versa. Free recall is less suitable because inter-item relationships exercise considerable influence on performance in free recall too. Kormi-Nouri (1995) does not address the question of a suitable testing method.

Another important point in Kormi-Nouri's assumptions is that he differentiates between the semantic integration of phrases and their familiarity. He considers familiarity as relating to word frequency. Semantic integration relates to the closeness of their pre-experimental association between verb and noun within a phrase independently of the frequency occurrence of the individual words. "Read the book" and "pick up the newspaper" are both "familiar" phrases, but they differ with regard to the semantic integration: "read" and "book" are closely associated, whereas "pick up" and "newspaper" are not.

What Kormi-Nouri (1995) calls semantic relationship has been varied by other authors too, under different names. Mohr (1992) speaks of associative relationships between verbs and object words. Engelkamp et al. (1993) speak of "bizarre" phrases (such as "paint the toothbrush"), and "normal" phrases (such as "smoke the pipe"). It is significant that also with these authors the phrases only differed in their "semantic" relationship, and not in the frequency of occurrence of the individual words. For simplicity's sake I will speak from now on of the "strength of association" between verbs and objects. In the experiments this is either high or low.

Unfortunately, the findings of the various studies are inconsistent. Despite the fact that it was observed in all the investigations (Engelkamp et al., 1993; Kormi-Nouri, 1995; Mohr, 1992) that higher strength of association between verb and object improved cued recall compared to lower strength of association, and despite an enactment effect being observed in all the investigations, Kormi-Nouri (1995) was the only one to observe the interaction he expected between the strength of association and encoding conditions. Engelkamp et al. (1993) and Mohr (1992) observed additive effects for encoding and association strength.

Before I look into the reasons for the different findings, a comparison of Kormi-Nouri's (1995) results in Exp. 2 with those of Engelkamp et al. (1993) in Exp. 3 would help to make things clearer.

Kormi-Nouri (1995) manipulated association strength, type of encoding, and type of cue (noun, verb). Because the type of cue did not interact with any of the other factors, I will not mention it further. After presentation of the learning list, subjects received first a free recall and then a cued recall test. The findings are summarised in Table 7.1.

The most significant result in the present context is the interaction between association strength and encoding condition: It was observed both in free recall and in cued recall; however, the differences showed opposite directions. In free recall the enactment effect was greater for strongly associated phrases than for weakly associated phrases. In cued recall it was greater for weakly than for strongly associated phrases. Kormi-Nouri (1995, p. 346) explains this unexpected three-way interaction by assuming that free recall "is a more effortful test, and therefore a combination of semantic and episodic integration is needed", whereas "in CR which is a less effortful test, episodic integration alone may produce the unitization effect."

TABLE 7.1

Relative performance in free recall (FR) and cued recall (CR) as a function of verb–object association and of the encoding condition (hearing, enactment) (Kormi-Nouri, 1995)

	Association Strength, FR		Association Strength, CR	
	High	*Low*	*High*	*Low*
Hearing	0.18	0.06	0.76	0.08
Enactment	0.49	0.27	0.87	0.38
Enactment effect	0.31	0.21	0.11	0.30

This posterior explanation assumes that information for semantic integration (high association strength) is particularly significant, or even only significant, if the test is difficult (as in free recall). However, in free recall it must be taken into account that recall is influenced by inter-item associations and by intra-phrase association. Cued recall should therefore be the better test for Kormi-Nouri's initial theory. Either way, it should also be expected in cued recall that the enactment effect be greater when the verb–object association is stronger than when it is weaker. At the most, this effect should be weaker in cued recall than in free recall. It should not be the other way round. Unfortunately, in his theoretical explanations before the experiments Kormi-Nouri left the question open as to which test they were supposed to apply.

The complexity of the processes occurring during free recall are also confirmed by unpublished data of ours. In various experiments, in which both strength of association and encoding conditions were manipulated, we were unable to observe any consistent effects in free recall. Neither was Helstrup (1993) able to observe any interaction between the two factors after the same variations. Due to the complexity of the processes involved in free recall I will not discuss Kormi-Nouri's findings on free recall any further.

The interaction in cued recall observed by Kormi-Nouri (1995) may be explained through ceiling effects (if cued recall after hearing is already 0.76 then there is only a maximum of 0.24 left for performance to increase to 1). Thus, it might be possible that his lists were too easy. Since he used the same lists in his three experiments it is hardly surprising that the patterns of findings on the experiments were consistent.

In their Exp. 3 Engelkamp et al. (1993) varied the strength of association and the encoding condition just as Kormi-Nouri (1995) did. They also varied a third factor which is not considered here. The object word was used as the cue for recalling the phrase. The results, summarised in Table 7.2, correspond with the expectation that encoding condition and strength of association are additive in cued recall. This "additivity" was replicated in two further experiments in this investigation as well as by Mohr (1992).

If the results of the two experiments reported in Tables 7.1 and 7.2 are compared, then two cells are of particular interest. With the strongly associated phrases, the performances were much better in Kormi-Nouri's investigation (0.76) than in Engelkamp et al's (0.57), and with the weakly associated phrases they were much poorer in Kormi-Nouri's investigation (0.08) than in Engelkamp et al's (0.28). The same applies to the other experiments in the two investigations. This means the possibility cannot be excluded that in Kormi-Nouri's investigations floor and ceiling effects are involved.

The question of the interactive or additive effect of the encoding condition and the strength of association between verb and object in action

TABLE 7.2
Relative performance in cued recall as a function of encoding
condition (hearing, enactment) and of strength of association
(Engelkamp, Zimmer, & Biegelmann, 1993, Exp. 3)

	Association Strength	
	High	Low
Hearing	0.57	0.28
Enactment	0.75	0.48
Enactment effect	0.18	0.20

phrases cannot be judged conclusively on the basis of the data available. None the less it may be recorded that verb–object association has an effect on cued recall both after hearing and after enactment. This is consistent with both theoretical positions. The multimodal theory is supported by the fact that additivity was observed in four experiments with different phrases and list lengths.

Up to now phrases and actions where the objects were an inherent component of the action have been considered. If a comparison were drawn between inherent and noninherent components of action phrases, also something could be found out about the episodic integration of action phrases. This consideration is dealt with shortly.

The investigations considered here have been restricted to verb–object phrases with transitive verbs, that is verbs that inherently involve an object. This may be illustrated by two examples: "bend" necessarily requires an object that is bent; "open" requires an object that is opened. Besides such obligatory components of action phrases there are also optional components. It is possible to open a door for someone, for example. The argument of the beneficiary of the action is not obligatory. It is a different matter in the phrase "get a theatre ticket for someone". In this case the beneficiary is just as obligatory as the object. The same goes for location details. In a statement such as "eat the bread in the train", the location information "in the train" is not obligatory. In a statement such as "take the shirt out of the cupboard", on the other hand, the location information is obligatory. This consideration shows that depending on the meaning of a verb in an action, certain components or arguments must be included in order to render the complete meaning of the action. It is assumed that these obligatory components belong to the action and that they are integrated by carrying out the action, independent of the pre-experimental associations. If carrying out an action therefore facilitates the integration of the meanings of actions, then obligatory or inherent location information should be integrated into the action more strongly through enactment than through just hearing. In this case location cues should be more effective after enactment than after hearing. On the other hand, location information which is not inherent to the actions should be integrated into the action more poorly through enactment than through hearing and especially through imagining them (cf. Chapter 5).

Engelkamp and Perrig (1986) tested both the assumption that obligatory location information is a more effective cue for a phrase after enactment than after imagining and the contrary assumption that optional location information is a more effective cue for a phrase after imagining than after enactment. To do this they had phrases learned with obligatory location information (such as "pick up the coin from the floor") and with optional location information (such as "do up one's shoes in the church") under enactment instructions and visual imagining instructions, and tested retention of the phrases by giving the location information as cues (e.g. "floor" or "church"). They found that the inherent location cues were more effective after enactment than after imagining, whereas the optional location cues were more effective after imagining than after enactment.

These results show once again that it is important to determine theoretically what belongs to an action and therefore is particularly well integrated and what does not belong to an action and therefore is more poorly integrated through enactment than through hearing or seeing.

Finally, it should be pointed out that Engelkamp et al. (1993) and Knopf and Neidhardt (1989) were able to observe an effect of association strength on recognition only after hearing and not after enactment. Hence, the findings also indicate that the effect of encoding processes on retention can only be explained reasonably if the different processes in the different retention tests are taken into consideration.

Direct and Concept-mediated Enactment

In the multimodal memory theory it is assumed that explicit retention requires conceptual information. Conceptual encoding takes place during enactment of an action because encoding of action phrases runs from the verbal input system via the conceptual system to the nonverbal motor output system. However, as described in Chapter 4, the multimodal memory theory also postulates a direct connection between the visual input system and the nonverbal motor output system. In other words, it distinguishes between a concept-mediated and a direct path of enactment (cf. also Engelkamp, 1991b). This distinction is also to be found in other contexts (cf. Prinz, 1987; Riddoch, Humphreys, & Price, 1989; Rothi, Ochipa, & Heilman, 1991).

The assumption of different paths leading to the performance of actions is also supported by neuropsychological findings. There are patients who can imitate actions better than they can perform them upon the verbal request to do so (De Renzi, Faglioni, & Sorgato, 1982; Heilman, 1973), and other patients who can perform actions upon being requested to but have difficulties imitating actions (Ochipa, Mothi, & Heilman, 1990).

As already made clear, in remembering action phrases concept-mediated enactment occurs if persons are verbally requested to perform tasks, as in the experiments on task performance previously described. The direct path occurs, for example, if someone imitates the movement of another person. It goes directly from the visual input to the motor output and bypasses the concept system. It is therefore expected that explicit retention is poorer after direct performance of an action than after concept-mediated performance of an action.

Zimmer and Engelkamp (1996) tested these assumptions in several experiments. In a first experiment they compared retention of phrases after hearing the phrases, after seeing the actions (without presentation of the phrases), and after imitating the actions seen (likewise without presentation of the phrases). Free recall was better after seeing and imitating than after hearing, but the additional performance of the action brought no improvement in retention compared to merely seeing the action. In a second experiment they used lists from Engelkamp and Zimmer (1983), so as to allow a comparison with the findings of this experiment. Again there was a seeing and an imitating condition, but performance of the action by the model was accompanied by the respective phrase for the action. The subject heard a phrase (e.g. "smoke the pipe") and then either only watched the model smoking the pipe (seeing) or additionally imitated the action (imitating). The seeing condition corresponded exactly to that of Engelkamp and Zimmer (1983). In addition, Engelkamp and Zimmer (1983) had also used a hearing and an enactment condition. The results of all three experiments are summarised in Table 7.3.

The findings show clearly that it makes no difference to the retention of actions seen and imitated whether the action is accompanied by a verbal

TABLE 7.3

Relative performance in free recall dependent on various encoding conditions (hearing, seeing, imitating, enactment) (Zimmer & Engelkamp, 1996, Exps. 1 and 2; Engelkamp & Zimmer, 1983)

	Encoding Condition			
	Hearing	Seeing	Imitating	Enactment
Experiment 1	0.26	0.42	0.44	–
Experiment 2	–	0.41	0.39	–
Engelkamp & Zimmer (1983)	0.25	0.39	–	0.54

phrase or not (comparison of Exp. 1 and 2). It is further shown that actions seen are recalled just as well as actions that are additionally imitated (Exp. 1 and 2). Although retention is better after seeing and imitating than after hearing (Engelkamp & Zimmer, 1983), it is even better if actions are performed upon request (Engelkamp & Zimmer, 1983).

In a further experiment, Zimmer and Engelkamp (1996) tried to make the imitating and enactment (on request) conditions even more similar by presenting the subjects with identical stimuli and by varying only the encoding sequence. This they achieved by varying the presentation sequence. Only the order of seeing and enactment was changed. Either the subjects heard the phrase, performed the action, and then saw the model, or they heard the phrase, saw the model, and imitated the action. In addition there were two conditions where after the phrase the action was either only seen or performed.

This experiment, too, showed that: (1) retention performance is no different following seeing and imitating; (2) retention is better after enactment than after imitating (and seeing); (3) seeing after enactment does not improve retention compared to enactment alone.

What is surprising is that adding the hearing condition to seeing and imitating the phrases seen does not change retention performance compared to merely seeing the actions. I attribute this finding to the same fact as leads to the lack of an elaboration effect after enactment. The nonverbal information made available through seeing the action is so effective that the additional verbal information made available through the phrase is ignored in recall.

What is more difficult to explain is the observation that actions that are only seen and those that are additionally performed are retained equally well. Although retention after imitating is poorer than after enactment, as expected, it is just as good as after merely seeing. I consider the explanation for this to be the fact that perceiving an action always leads to encoding of the action concept. The subjects automatically categorise the movement they see as an action. Imitation of the action seen takes place additionally and directly, without being mediated via the action concept. However, this direct sensory-motor processing is not used in free recall, only the action concepts are used in free recall.

With this in mind it is possible also to explain the finding that retention performances for phrases enacted upon verbal request are better than for phrases that are imitated. If an action is performed based on a verbal phrase, then the action concept must be encoded. If an action seen is imitated, then no activation of the action concept is necessary for imitating, although it is assumed that the concept of the action is also encoded due to the perception of the action. What is important, however, is that in this case the action concept is not used as a basis performing the action. On the contrary, enactment is controlled directly via perception of the movement. Performing the action is not tied to the action concept. In this case, retention is only based on conceptual encoding through perception of the action.

The last question to be explained is why additional seeing after enactment does not improve retention compared to enactment alone. These findings can be explained in a similar way to the lack of effect of hearing in addition to seeing. In the latter case, seeing is already so effective that the verbal information is not used in recall. In the former case, enactment is already so effective that the visual information is not used in recall. It again becomes clear that, aside from the encoding, it is which information is used in a recall test that is critical.

DIFFERENTIATIONS IN RETRIEVAL PROCESSES

It has already become clear that in different retention tests use is made of different information encoded during the learning phase. The specific mechanisms used in the processing of different retention tests, and their dependence on the encoding conditions of hearing and enactment, are the subject of this section.

The Serial Position Curve in Free Recall

It was already assumed in the generation-recognition models that two processes are responsible for free recall. It was postulated that the generation process is based on relational information and the process of recognition on item-specific information (Einstein & Hunt, 1980; Hunt & Einstein, 1981). In the multimodal memory theory, this relational information is specified as categorical-relational information, and it is assumed that it is no different after hearing or enactment and that the enactment effect is therefore due to better item-specific encoding through enactment (e.g. Zimmer, 1991; Zimmer & Engelkamp, 1989a).

Yet there were findings which did not fit into this picture. Cohen (1981), for example, made the early observation that in the serial position curve after enactment the recency effect was observed, but not the primacy effect. At first this was explained by the assumption that the primacy effect was due to the fact that in particular the items in the first positions on the lists are often rehearsed during learning (e.g. Rundus, 1971). These items would therefore be easier to generate and to recognise. Since the encoding of actions through enactment is assumed to be strategy-free (Cohen, 1985; Kausler, 1989), the first items in enactment should not be rehearsed more than other items and so no primacy effect should occur. This explanation does not explain why then an enactment effect is observed.

The fact that with longer lists the primacy effect also occurs after enactment is another point that does not fit in well with the assumption of strategy-free encoding through enactment. Zimmer analysed the serial position curves for experiments carried out by Zimmer, Engelkamp, Mohr, and Mohr (1988) and Mohr et al. (1989) at a later stage. The lists comprised 48 and 80 phrases, respectively. Primacy and recency effects were shown both after hearing and enactment. Besides this, a comparison of the position curves showed that the enactment effect was limited to the second half of the list.

These results not only change the way the serial position curves for hearing and enactment are regarded, but also demand a different conception of the processes occurring during free recall. At first the only thing that was noticed was that no primacy effect was observed after enactment. The recency effect and the heights of the curves were not even considered. Attention was only brought to differences in the recency effect after the long lists had been analysed. The recency effect proved to be greater after enactment than hearing (it was steeper and extended over more positions) and to be the decisive source for the overall enactment effect.

Zimmer et al. (1997) investigated this interesting observation further in another study. In their first experiment they varied the list length from 12 through 24 to 36 phrases and compared the serial position curves after hearing and enactment. Their findings are shown in Fig. 7.1. A comparison of the serial position curves over the different list lengths shows clearly that the enactment effect comes about in the latter part of the lists. The recency effect is much steeper after enactment than after hearing. On the other hand, although a stronger primacy effect is shown after hearing, hearing has no retention superiority even at the beginning of the lists.

A further experiment with a very long list of 80 items showed the same basic results. The enactment effect primarily emerges in the latter part of the list. The recency effect is more extended and steeper after enactment than after hearing. A comparable, small primacy effect is shown both after hearing and enactment (Fig. 7.2).

What do these findings reveal about the processes in free recall after hearing and enactment? The idea that free recall is based on generating and recognising items is inadequate in order to explain the findings on the serial position curve after hearing and enactment. This is above all true of the primacy effect. But also the explanation of the recency effect, which is often ascribed to the short-term acoustic memory and which should therefore be restricted to just a few positions at the end of the list (e.g. Glanzer & Cunitz, 1966; Rundus, 1971), does not fit in with the properties of the serial position curve observed after enactment. This is clearly inaccurate with regard to the recency effect after enactment. The serial position curve in free recall should be clearly distinguished from the one in serial recall (Oloffson, 1996).

In order to explain these findings, therefore, other mechanisms must be sought. Lockhart, Craik, and Jacoby (1976) had already suggested distin-

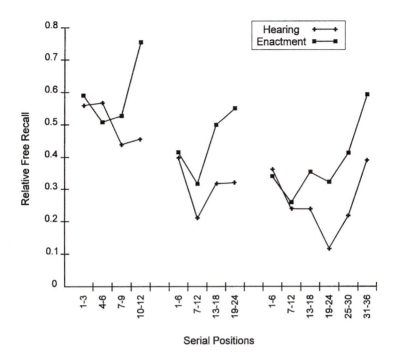

FIG. 7.1.   Serial position curves in free recall as a function of the encoding condition (hearing, enactment) and of list length (12, 24, 36 items) (Zimmer, Helstrup, Engelkamp, & Saathoff, 1997, Exp. 1).

guishing between two mechanisms in free recall. One corresponds to the generation-recognition theories of free recall. Items must first be generated before they can be recognised as elements of the learning episode. Lockhart et al. (1976) call this reconstruction of episodic information. They also postulate a recall mechanism that can be achieved with item-specific information alone. It is assumed that after learning an episode, part of the items in this episode are accessed "directly", without a generating process. It is assumed that upon overall reactivation of the episode a number of items "spring to mind" directly. Their activation level is so high that they are directly accessed and recognised as being "old". It is also assumed that in direct access "looking at the episode" ensues more or less from behind, from the end frontwards (cf. also Zimmer, 1991).

This direct access is basically a function of item-specific encoding. This in turn is better after enactment is mainly responsible for the extended recency effect in free recall after enactment.

In the case of reconstruction, however, the generation-recognition models assume that items are generated along inter-item associations. Previously

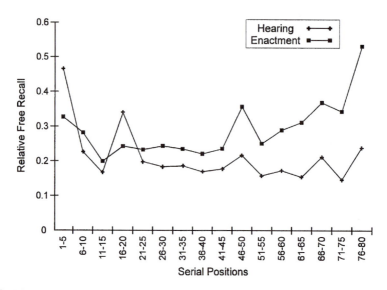

FIG. 7.2.   Serial position curve for a very long list (80 items) after hearing and enactment (Zimmer, Helstrup, Engelkamp, & Saathoff, 1997, Exp. 2).

generated items serve as cues for other items (cf. Raaijmakers & Shiffrin, 1981). Once the items are generated, the item-specific information is used to decide whether they are "old". Since the items from the beginning of the list are particularly intensively rehearsed, their probability of being generated and recognised is particularly high—which would explain the primacy effect.

If this is the case, why then is there no primacy effect after enactment with short lists whereas there is one with long lists? This finding can be explained by the fact that the mechanism of direct access is not adequate for recall with long lists. With short lists recall performance after enactment is almost entirely due to direct access, which is why there is little or no primacy effect here. After hearing the item-specific information is poorer. That is why direct access is less effective. The items are reconstructed instead, and this leads to the primacy effect. If the learning list is longer, then at some time a point is reached where direct access alone is no longer effective enough even after enactment. At that point reconstruction is made use of even after enactment, and a primacy effect is shown even after enactment.

An interesting but open question is whether the efficiency of these two mechanisms underlying free recall (reconstruction and direct access) decrease differentially over time (cf. Knopf, 1991, 1992; Nilsson, Cohen, & Nyberg, 1989).

The overall result is that: (1) performances in free recall can be due to two different mechanisms (reconstruction and direct access), (2) due to the different encoding processes after hearing and enactment different use is made of these mechanisms after hearing and enactment, and (3) the employment of these two mechanisms after enactment also depends on the list length. The idea that different systems are involved in recollection is included in this concept of free recall. The specific assumption is that insofar as it is due to direct access, free recall benefits from the motor information.

The Effect of Levels of Processing in Free Recall

In memory experiments with verbal material the effect of levels of processing has often been replicated (Craik & Tulving, 1975; Lockhart & Craik, 1990). "Shallow" processing leads to poorer retention performances than "deep" processing. Up until recently, however, it has been unclear as to whether this levels of processing effect also occurs after SPTs. We know that it is extremely difficult to increase retention performance after enactment through explicit elaboration instructions (Cohen, 1981; Helstrup, 1987; Lichty et al. 1988; Nilsson & Cohen, 1988; Zimmer, 1984). We explained this with the assumption that the item-specific information made available through enactment is already so good that additional information is not made use of.

Can retention performance after enactment be impeded by instructions to produce "shallow" encoding? Few investigation have gone into this question. Cohen (1981) tried to achieve "shallow" encoding through questions such as "How much noise does an action produce?", and "deep" encoding through questions such as "How often is this action performed in daily life?". Cohen found a levels of processing effect after hearing, but not after enactment. However, Cohen's questions related to physical aspects of actions and not to linguistic aspects of phrases.

The levels of processing in the classical sense was only manipulated after enactment by Nilsson and Craik (1990, Exp. 3). They compared a deep conceptual orienting task with a shallow task orientated to the linguistic surface (counting letters or syllables), both for hearing and enactment. They observed a clear effect of levels of processing after hearing and a substantially reduced effect of levels of processing after enactment. (It remains unclear whether the effect is still significant after enactment). These findings contrast with those reported by Zimmer (1992). He observed clear effects of levels of processing both after hearing and enactment.

Therefore Zimmer and Engelkamp (in press) systematically investigated the question of whether an effect of levels of processing was to be observed after enactment. Besides the depth of processing and the encoding, they varied the length of the lists to be learned, because Nilsson and Craik (1990) had worked with short lists and Zimmer (1992) with relatively long lists.

Zimmer and Engelkamp (in press) carried out 6 experiments altogether. The experiments mainly differed in list length (ranging from 12 to 96 items). Besides a conceptual orienting task (how probable is the action x in the situation y, e.g. spreading something on bread—at the breakfast table?), a "shallow" orienting task was used (subjects had to judge whether a certain sequence of letters occurred in the phrase). Otherwise the subjects had to either only listen to the phrase (hearing) or additionally carry it out (enactment). The encoding condition was varied between the subjects. In those experiments, learning was incidental.

The results reveal a clear pattern of free recall. First, even after enactment an effect of levels of processing is found if the lists contain 48 or more phrases. Second, even if an effect of levels of processing is observed after enactment (0.13), this is smaller than after hearing (0.25). Third, with short lists (between 12 and 24 phrases) there is an effect of levels of processing after hearing (0.20) but not after enactment (0.03). Fourth, the usual enactment effect only occurs after "shallow" processing, not after "deep" processing.

We had assumed that good item-specific encoding is brought about automatically by enactment under all conditions (with shallow and deep levels of processing). For this reason, recall ought to be independent of the orienting tasks after enactment. This assumption is not confirmed by the current findings. An effect of levels of processing is shown with long lists, against expectation. How can this effect be explained?

This effect is probably mainly due to the instructions for "shallow" processing, since the variation of list length primarily affects this and since other investigations have shown that manipulation of elaboration, that is differing degrees of "deep" processing, has no effect on free recall after enactment (e.g. Cohen, 1981; Nilsson & Cohen, 1988; Zimmer, 1984). Since the "shallow" orienting task relates to the processing of linguistic aspects of the phrases, and enactment instructions relate to the action concept and its enactment, two different tasks are required, which lead to two different memory traces under enactment. In particular episodic-relational encoding through enactment could be disrupted by the linguistic orienting task, since this is inserted between two enactments and makes establishing an association between them even more difficult.

This would also explain the influence of list length. Since recall of long lists is largely governed by reconstruction, relational information is necessary for recall of longer lists. It is precisely the encoding of this information that would be disrupted by the "shallow" orienting task. Direct access is sufficient for recall of shorter lists after enactment. This is why the "shallow" orienting task has no effect here (compared with the "deep" one).

The situation is somewhat different under the hearing condition. Instructions for "deep" processing improve both conceptual item-specific encoding and relational encoding and so increase retention performance after hearing to the level of performance after enactment. It should be emphasised again that "deep" processing instructions influence retention not after enactment but after hearing.

"Shallow" processing instructions draw the attention to the linguistic aspects of the phrase and hinder conceptual encoding. Unlike the enactment condition, activation of the action concept through the "shallow" instructions under the hearing condition is almost completely disrupted because there are no specific instructions for encoding the action concept (cf. Chapter 6). Consequently, instructions for "shallow" encoding bring recall of long lists to an almost complete standstill. Hardly anything is reproduced.

The fact that despite poor encoding of the action concepts, recall of short lists is still achieved after hearing could be due to the fact that direct access also occurs here, using the "linguistic" information in the hearing condition.

Either way, at this point it can be stated that the simple idea of free recall as a product of generation and recognition is inadequate to explain the findings.

The Effect of Levels of Processing in Recognition Memory

It is generally assumed that item-specific information is more critical for recognition than relational information (e.g. Engelkamp et al., 1998; Hunt & Einstein, 1981; McDaniel, Einstein, Dunay, & Cobb, 1986). In the context of verbal learning, only one type of item-specific information is usually allowed for, due to the mere fact that only verbal learning is studied. In the present context, however, we distinguish between conceptual item-specific information and motor item-specific information in the processing of action phrases through enactment. If this item-specific conceptual and motor information is responsible for the good recognition after enactment, then there should be no levels of processing effect on recognition after enactment. According to the literature (e.g. Craik & Tulving, 1975), a clear effect of levels of processing is to be expected after hearing.

In the experiments on processing depth described in the previous section, the recall tests were each followed by a recognition test. The results of these recognition tests showed no effect of levels of processing after enactment and no list length effect. As expected after hearing, a clear effect of levels of processing is shown in recognition too. It also covaries very little with the list length. The fact that recall and recognition memory are not correlated after SPTs was also observed in other studies (e.g. Svensson & Nilsson, 1989).

The point is that more precise ascertainment of the item-specific information must be taken into account not only in free recall but also in recognition memory.

The Effect of Word Frequency in Recognition Memory

In the enactment condition, an action phrase or action verb is usually given first and the action is then carried out. In the system approach this means that the verbal input system is also involved in processing during enactment. Up to now little attention was paid to this aspect because the verbal input system is equally involved with hearing or with enactment and can be treated as a constant in comparing hearing and enactment. It should also hold for the verbal input system that the processes of this system should influence retention independently of the processes of the conceptual or motor system. It is therefore desirable to test the degree to which a variable that manipulates the processes in the verbal input system takes effect independently of the enactment effect.

Word frequency seems a reasonable choice for investigating this question. The word frequency effect consists of infrequent words being recognised better than frequent ones. It is assumed that this effect is due to processes in the linguistic input system, that is the mental lexicon (Mandler et al., 1982). This assumption is supported by the fact that manipulations that are normally based on the conceptual system, such as semantic elaboration (Mandler et al., 1982), concreteness (Gorman, 1961; Paivio & Olver, 1964), and generation (Gardiner et al., 1988), have no influence on the word frequency effect. The findings supported the assumption that word frequency influences recognition memory independently of variables that are considered to be conceptual, and they are compatible with the assumption that the word frequency effect is based on lexical information.

It follows for retention after enactment that if lexical information contributes to retention after enactment, then recognition after enactment should be better with infrequent verbs than with frequent verbs. If this influence is independent of conceptual and motor information, then the verb frequency effect should also be independent of the enactment effect.

In order to investigate these assumptions, Engelkamp, Zimmer, and Kurbjuweit (1995) had frequent and infrequent action verbs learned under hearing and enactment conditions and tested recognition with the verbs. The results are summarised in Table 7.4.

As expected, two main effects are shown, and no interaction. Infrequent verbs are recognised better than frequent ones. Independently of this effect, recognition is better after enactment than after hearing. This pattern of findings supports the assumption that the basis for the verb frequency effect is to be found in the lexicon and the basis for the enactment effect in the motor system. Overall it becomes clear that in recognition memory it must be taken into account which subsystems are used in each particular case.

TABLE 7.4
Relative performance in recognition (Pr score) as a function of verb
frequency and of encoding condition (Engelkamp, Zimmer, & Kurbjuweit,
1995, Exp. 2)

	Verb Frequency		
Encoding Condition	Frequent	Infrequent	Verb Frequency Effect
Hearing	0.46	0.61	0.15
Enactment	0.65	0.80	0.15
Enactment effect	0.19	0.19	–

Conscious Versus Familiarity-based Recognition Memory

Two mechanisms (retrieval-based and familiarity-based recognition) have repeatedly (e.g. Jacoby, 1991; Jacoby & Dallas, 1981; Mandler, 1980; Tulving, 1985) been postulated as forming the basis of recognition, independently of the differentiation between lexical, conceptual, and motor item-specific information introduced here. In retrieval-based recognition, subjects can remember the episodic context corresponding to an item. In familiarity-based recognition, subjects only have "the feeling" that an item belongs to the learning list. Jacoby (1991; Jacoby, Toth, Yonelinas, & Debner, 1994) calls retrieval-based recognition controlled and conscious, and familiarity-based recognition automatic and unconscious, without restricting this comment by relating it to the episodic context. Taking this differentiation into consideration, the question arises as to whether recognition after enactment is automatic or controlled. According to the multimodal memory theory after encoding through enactment, retrieval-based recognition should be more probable than familiarity-based recognition (cf. Chapters 5 and 6). At the same time, there should be more retrieval-based recognition after enactment than after hearing.

In the remember–know technique, subjects are instructed to state whether they remember the episodic context of the item ("remember") or whether the item "only" seems familiar to them ("know"). This procedure goes back to Tulving (1985) and Gardiner (1988). Since an item can only be positioned as remembered or familiar, "remember" and "know" judgements are disjunctive.

In the process-dissociation technique devised by Jacoby (1991), retrieval-based recognition is subject to intentional control. Jacoby uses this characteristic of controlled recognition to reveal automatic recognition. Automatic and controlled processes can be separated by creating two different test situations. In one, both processes take effect in the same direction, while in the other they take effect in different directions. Jacoby implemented these two situations by presenting two learning lists in the learning phase and manipulating the test instructions. In the "inclusion" condition the subjects are to refer to the items on both lists as "old". The performance here is based on both automatic and controlled recollection processes.

In the "exclusion" condition the subjects are instructed to refer only to the items from List 2 as "old". Items from List 1 are to be called "new". All the items on List 1 that are still called "old" are "false alarms" according to these instructions. Under this condition, an item is then only erroneously called "old" if it is familiar and not remembered.

Both methods, the remember–know method and the process dissociation technique, have been applied to recognition after hearing and enactment. In two experiments by Engelkamp and Dehn (1997), subjects had to learn 80 and 120 phrases intentionally under hearing and enactment conditions. Recognition was tested with the remember–know technique. Subjects marked the items they had called "old" as "remember" when they remembered any details of the learning situation, or as "know" when they remembered when they just knew that the item was "old". Both experiments showed the same pattern. The enactment effect was due to the "remember" responses. More "remember" responses were made after enactment than after hearing. The "know" answers are given more seldom after enactment because they are complementary to the "remember" responses.

The "remember–know" technique has been criticised because guessing processes are not taken into consideration in the know answers (e.g. Strack & Bless, 1994). They form a rest category. However, this critique is irrelevant for the assumption that recognition after enactment is mainly retrieval-based.

The process-dissociation procedure was also applied by Engelkamp and Dehn (1997). In this experiment, subjects learned two lists. The first list was learned incidentally. The phrases were either read aloud or enacted by the subjects. The second list was learned intentionally. Here the phrases were presented acoustically and listened to. Items of both lists mixed with distractor items were later presented in a recognition test. In the recognition test, subjects were either allocated to the inclusion condition. In this case, they had to judge any item as "old" that belonged to List 1 or List 2. Or they were allocated to the exclusion condition. In this case, they were requested to mark only those items as "old" that belonged to List 2. Table 7.5 summarises the old-answers for the different item types and test conditions.

The findings make four points clear. (1) Recognition for hearing (List 2) and the false alarms with the distractors do not differ dependent on the test condition. In other words, performance for the items on List 1 under both test conditions are not subject to different response biases. (2) The usual enactment effect occurs under the inclusion condition. Items are recognised

TABLE 7.5
Probabilities of calling an item "old", as a function of item type and test type
(Engelkamp & Dehn, 1997)

| | Item Type | | | |
| | List 1 | | List 2 | |
Test Type	Enactment	Reading	Hearing	Distractor
Inclusion	0.86	0.58	0.63	0.21
	Correct	Correct	Correct	FA
Exclusion	0.26	0.39	0.61	0.28
	FA	FA	Correct	FA

Note: Items from List 1 which had been read and enacted were to be called "old" in the inclusion and "new" in the exclusion condition. FA stands for false alarms.

better after enactment than after reading. (3) Under the exclusion condition, only the items heard were to be called "old". If items from List 1 were therefore called "old", then this was a false alarm. Such false alarms are more frequent after reading than after enactment. (4) If the differences between correct answers (inclusion) and false alarms (exclusion) are calculated for enactment and reading, an estimate is obtained for the items recognised in a controlled way. The proportion of these items is 0.60 after enactment and 0.19 after reading. These findings correspond with the results of the remember–know experiments. Controlled recognition is better after enactment than after reading.

If the formula for estimating the automatic proportions according to Jacoby (1991) is applied here, a value of 0.65 is found for automatic recognition after enactment and 0.48 after reading. In other words, automatic recognition is also greater after enactment than after reading.

Also with the process-dissociation technique, there is the problem that guessing is not taken into account (Graf & Komatsu, 1994). However, Dehn and Engelkamp (1997) demonstrated that the same pattern of findings was observed when guessing was taken into account.

It can be concluded from these investigations that recognition after enactment (compared to hearing or reading) primarily favours retrieval-based recognition. But automatic recognition also occurs, after hearing/ reading and after enactment. Interpretation of the findings on automatic recognition, however, depends decisively on whether it is assumed that recognition judgement can be retrieval-based and familiarity-based at the same time (as in Jacoby's 1991 assumption of independence)—or not, as postulated by Gardiner (1988) with his assumption of exclusivity (cf. Dehn & Engelkamp, 1997).

Summary

With regard to the processes behind free recall it is not sufficient to see recall as the generation and recognition of items but that direct access to items must also be taken into account. It is direct access which distinguishes recall after enactment from recall after hearing. The reason for better direct access after enactment than after hearing is that enactment makes both conceptual and motor information available in combined form.

Recognition also turns out to be more complicated than initially supposed. It is not enough to assume *one* type of information and *one* type of process. Both the information and the processes behind the recognition must be differentiated. In principle, verbal, conceptual and motor information can be used for recognition. After enactment, it appears that conceptual and motor information are primarily used. Which information is used depends decisively on how well it contributes, in the concrete case, to discrimination between "old" and "new" items. With regard to the processes behind recognition, a distinction must be made between retrieval-based (controlled) and familiarity-based (automatic) recognition. It has been shown that recognition is more strongly based on controlled processes after enactment than after hearing. Whether the automatic processes in recognition differ after enactment and hearing is less clear.

Although I have tried to present the complications involved in explaining separately the enactment effect for encoding in the learning phase and for the retrieval processes in the test phase, it has become increasingly apparent that this is not completely possible, because the processes of encoding and retrieval interact in a complex way.

RETENTION IN THE INTERPLAY OF ENCODING AND RETRIEVAL

To a certain degree, the results observed in the investigation into remembering linguistic material (Chapter 2) repeat themselves in the investigation of the enactment effect. The first attempt to explain retention regarded it as a function of encoding. Once it turned out that the retention phenomena concerned could not be explained adequately this way, attention was turned to the processes in retrieval too. It was only after no adequate explanation could be found here either that the interplay of both processes was taken into consideration.

Similarly, in research on the enactment effect, interest was focused first on the encoding processes, then on retrieval processes, and finally on their interplay. However, this interplay has proved to be highly complex in the enactment effect. This is due to the facts that: (1) with regard to encoding and retrieval processes, more aspects are differentiated than item-specific and relational information as well as two or three code systems, and (2) it is no longer assumed that a certain test is based on a single mechanism, which always falls back on the same information, but that in one and the same test different mechanisms can take effect, using different types of information.

It has become apparent that the principle of encoding specificity, which is already made complicated by the stronger differentiation of the encoding processes, becomes more complicated because in one and the same retention test different retrieval mechanisms can be used.

If the differentiated assumptions on encoding and retrieval are applied to retention after enactment, then it becomes clear that the situation is even more complicated. This is due to the fact that factors such as material properties and encoding instructions, which are aimed at influencing item-specific and relational information, have a different effect under enactment than under hearing. That means, for example, that encoding instructions aimed at the linguistic surface have a different influence on item-specific encoding under the hearing condition than under enactment, or that instructions aimed at pair integration have a different effect on episodic-relational encoding under the imagining condition than under enactment. Technically speaking, this means that the encoding specificity does not take effect in a two-way interaction between encoding instructions (or stimulus material) and retention test, but in a three-way interaction which includes additionally the factor of hearing (or imagining) versus enactment.

Effects of Levels of Processing and List Length

I have previously reported on a series of experiments where Zimmer and Engelkamp (in press) reported on the influence of processing depth and list length on free recall and on recognition after hearing and enactment.

In the present context the findings on the list lengths of 48 to 96 are summarised. They represent the findings for "long" lists. The findings for "short" lists relate to the list length of 24 phrases. I have left the extremely short lists out, because the level of retention performance is much higher in this case than in all the other list lengths. The findings are summarised in Table 7.6.

In this example the findings reveal a four-way interaction. This is due to the fact that list length was varied in addition to processing depth. In deep processing neither hearing/enactment nor list length has an effect. The only effect found is that performance is better in recognition than in free recall. In shallow processing, however, there is great variation in performance, which proves to be dependent on the interplay between hearing/enactment and list length on the one hand and test type on the other. In recognition, performance is only better after enactment than after hearing. In free recall it is also better with short lists than with long ones. Finally, it is shown that there

TABLE 7.6

Relative performance in free recall and in recognition (correct answers) after hearing and enactment as a function of levels of processing (deep, shallow) and list length (long, short) (Zimmer & Engelkamp, in press)

Test Type	Free Recall		Recognition	
	Deep	Shallow	Deep	Shallow
Long lists				
Hearing	0.30	0.05	0.86	0.43
Enactment	0.31	0.18	0.91	0.80
Short lists				
Hearing	0.34	0.15	0.85	0.47
Enactment	0.32	0.29	0.94	0.89

is a levels of processing effect after hearing under all conditions, but after enactment there is only such an effect in free recall with long lists.

This pattern of findings not only proves that the interplay of encoding and retrieval is complex, but also shows that factors influencing these two processes do so in different ways under the hearing and enactment conditions.

Effects of Integration of Unrelated Verb Pairs

In Chapter 5 I reported on experiments concerning the differential quality of the episodic-relational encoding of pairs of unrelated action verbs after hearing, imagining and enactment. In these experiments (e.g. Engelkamp, 1986a, 1986b) action phrases were tested in free recall and cued recall in the paradigm of pair-associate learning. It was expected that the episodic-relational encoding of action pairs through enactment would be difficult compared to hearing and especially to imagining. Accordingly, the performance in cued recall after enactment would be particularly poor. But, in free recall, performance would be very good after enactment (as in list learning) and better than after hearing or imagining, because item-specific encoding is very good after enactment. These expectations were confirmed.

Here, too, it can be further shown that this pattern is modulated by further encoding instructions, leading to three-way interaction. Explicit instructions for episodic-relational encoding have a different effect under the hearing or imagining condition to that under enactment, and the effect differs in free recall and in cued recall.

Basically, the multimodal memory theory leads to the expectation that the essentially poor episodic-relational encoding through enactment is not improved to any significant degree even if the subjects are given explicit instructions to integrate the pairs. With hearing and especially with imagining, however, such instructions would improve even further the epi-sodic-relational encoding, which is already good. These assumptions have not yet been tested in a single experiment, but they are supported by findings obtained on the one hand with noun pairs under hearing and imagining conditions (e.g. Begg, 1983) and on the other with verb pairs under enact-ment (Engelkamp et al., 1991).

In pair-associate learning experiments with pairs of unrelated nouns, for example, it was shown that interactive imagining instructions led to better performances in cued recall than separate imagining instructions. Free recall, however, was influenced little by variation of these instructions. At the same time, interactive instructions led to much higher cued recall than free recall instructions (Begg, 1983; Marschark & Hunt, 1989; Marschark & Surian, 1989).

This pattern differs greatly from the one observed after instructions for separate and integrative processing of the pair items in SPTs. Both kinds of instructions have little influence on performance in free recall. But under the integrative instructions, performance in cued recall is (1) only slightly higher than under separate instructions, and (2) lower than that in free recall in all cases (Engelkamp et al., 1991).

Thus, even though it has not been tested in a single experiment, three-way interaction exists in pair associated learning, too, between encoding (sepa-rate vs. integrative instructions), retrieval (free recall vs. cued recall), and condition (hearing or imagining vs. enactment).

Effects of the Bizarreness of Phrases

Another example of how a two-way interaction between encoding and retrieval leads to a three-way interaction is given by the additional manip-ulation of the bizarreness of the phrases. In several experiments Engelkamp et al. (1993) had normal phrases (e.g. "smoke the pipe") and bizarre phrases (e.g. "saw the pipe in two") memorised under hearing and enactment con-ditions and tested retention for the phrases either in a recognition test or in a cued recall test where the object words in the phrases (e.g. "pipe") were used as the cues. The findings of this investigation are summarised in Fig. 7.3 for the conditions "immediate retention test" and "no disruption during retention testing".

This interaction will be explained in detail, since it sheds light on the role of the verbal input system and its different functions in hearing and enactment on the one hand and in recognition and cued recall for phrases via phrase parts on the other.

In these experiments, verbal information was manipulated. It was not the frequency of the individual words that was varied, but the frequency of the common occurrence of the verb and the object of a phrase, that is their

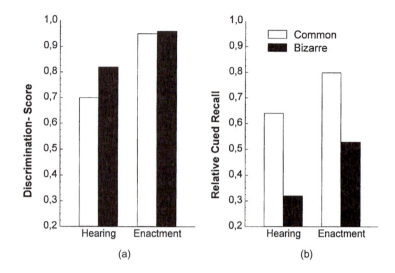

FIG. 7.3.   Performance in (a) recognition and (b) cued recall for bizarre and normal action phrases after hearing and enactment (Exps. 1 and 3, Engelkamp, Zimmer, & Biegelmann, 1993; the two experiments only differ in test type).

strength of association. With bizarre phrases this association strength is zero. Verb and object had practically never occurred in this combination. With the normal phrases, the association strength is high, that is verb and object occur together often. The frequency of occurrence of the phrase parts (object and verb) was controlled.

In cued recall the subjects are presented with the object words as cues and have to remember the verb that belongs to it. The verbs must be sought for given objects. I presume that this searching process takes place in the lexicon (to be more precise, under the influence of the lexicon in the conceptual system) and that the more strongly associated object and verb are, the more successful this search is. This mechanism should be equally effective after hearing and enactment and should be responsible for the fact that common phrases are recalled better than bizarre phrases. If a phrase is generated in this way then the decision is taken as to whether it is "old". After enactment, unlike hearing, not only conceptual information but also motor information is available for this decision. In other words, two independent effects are expected in cued recall—and are observed.

In recognition the subjects are presented with whole phrases. They merely have to decide whether the phrases are "old". After enactment they can use the conceptual and the motor information directly. Since this information is very good after enactment they make no use of the lexical information. The situation is different after hearing. Here the subjects do not have the motor information that they have carried out a task. Thus after hearing, the information on the association strengths in the lexicon is helpful. The subjects therefore use this information after hearing. It is assumed that presenting the unusual links between verbs and objects in the bizarre phrases leads to a more distinctive memory trace than presenting common connections in the common phrases. Therefore, bizarre phrases are better recognised than common phrases after hearing.

Effects of Verb Frequency

We have already seen that the frequency of verbs influences recognition independently of the encoding condition (hearing, enactment). Both factors have an additive effect. As usual, the enactment effect was attributed to the quality of the conceptual and motor item-specific information. The effect of verb frequency was explained by variations in information in the lexicon.

Interestingly, there is another memory effect which depends on word frequency: the effect of word repetition in implicit memory tests. It was shown in several studies that in word identification tasks, the repetition effect or repetition priming is greater for infrequent words than for frequent words (Forbach, Stanners, & Hochhaus, 1974; Kinoshita, 1989; Roediger, Weldon, Stadler, & Riegler 1992). Performance in such word identification tasks is independent both of the meaning of the word and of the instructions, which manipulate conceptual processing (Boles, 1983; Hines, 1976; Shanon, 1979). This means that word identification is independent of conceptual encoding. Studying the repetition effect dependent on verb frequency after hearing and enactment thus opens a second possibility of testing the independence of the enactment effect of the effect of information in the lexicon. If conceptual information plays no role in word identification, then motor information certainly should not, and performance in word identification should be no different after hearing or enactment. It should, however, be better for infrequent verbs than for frequent verbs. Apart from this, a repetition effect should occur which depends on word frequency but not on the encoding condition.

In order to test these assumptions, Engelkamp et al. (1995) tested half of the verbs in the experiment described earlier in a recognition test and half in a word identification test. In summary, there were two main findings: (1) The enactment effect and the verb frequency effect are independent of each other in recognition. (2) There is no enactment effect in word identification but there is a repetition effect which depends on verb frequency. I consider this pattern of findings as evidence for the assumption that the basis of the verb frequency effect should be sought in the lexicon and not in the conceptual system and that the enactment effect is due to conceptual and motor information and not to lexical information.

CHAPTER EIGHT

Theoretical integration III: Inclusion of retrieval processes

EFFECTS OF ENCODING

The most important new findings on encoding concern the relationships between components of action phrases and the direct link from the visual input system to the nonverbal motor output system.

The assumptions on item-specific and relational encoding have been further differentiated. This differentiation concerns the transfer of the term "relational information" to the encoding of an individual action. The encoding of an individual action is no longer regarded as purely item-specific but as a combined unit, which permits the relational encoding of its parts. Both the actions themselves and the objects they are applied to are considered as prototype parts of actions. The differentiation between action and object is reflected in action phrases in the differentiation between action verb and object word. The associations between verb and object word as well as between action concept and object concept differ in closeness, depending on the frequency of experience. They are pre-experimental components of the verbal and the conceptual system.

These verb–object associations can therefore be interpreted completely analogously to the categorical-relational information between actions. Their processing should be no different to the categorical-relational encoding between phrases after hearing and enactment.

A further differentiation arises with regard to verb–object associations to be established for the first time during the learning episode. In analogy with learning new associations between unrelated actions, it is a matter of episodic-relational encoding processes. In enactment, this episodic-relational encoding between actions and their objects is exactly the opposite of that between actions. While focusing on information relevant to the action through enactment impedes the establishment of associations between unrelated actions, it promotes it between actions and their objects because both are relevant to the respective action. In fact, this is also true of other parts within phrases insofar as they are relevant to the action. For example, in actions that lead to a change in the location of the object (such as "throw the apple out of the window"), the location information can also be relevant to the action. Parts relevant to the action do not, however, include such location information as is related to an action by coincidence (such as "eat the apple on the train"). To summarise, then, when considering episodic-relational encoding within phrases it is essential to check whether or not part of the information to be associated is relevant to the action.

The findings on the direct link between the visual input system and the motor output system, on the other hand, were expected, due to the theoretical assumptions. In the multimodal memory theory it was assumed that imitating an action seen would make poorer information on the action concept available than performing the same action upon verbal presentation of the phrase. This expectation was confirmed. It was also shown, however, that retention of an imitated action was equal to that of an action that had only been seen. Besides this, retention was better in both cases than after hearing action phrases (Zimmer & Engelkamp, 1996). Due to these findings it was assumed that action concepts are also activated when actions are seen and imitated, but that imitating does not make use of the action concepts. It is rather the sequence of physical movements or partial movements that are imitated than a complete action. In a way, imitating an action is comparable to spelling a word. The overall stimulus is separated into parts. With a verbal request for an action it is different: The action is planned and carried out as a whole, just like naming an object is based on the planning and pronunciation of a whole word. This is why performing an action after presentation of an action phrase promotes retention but imitating an action seen does not. It does not lead to better encoding of the action concept than merely seeing the action.

EFFECTS OF RETRIEVAL

The main contribution of the experiments reported in Chapter 7 concerns the retrieval processes. This contribution shall now be shown successively for different test procedures.

Retrieval Processes in Free Recall

It has been shown repeatedly that the serial position curves in free recall differ after hearing and enactment. After enactment there is often no primacy effect in the serial position curve, and the recency effect is more marked after enactment than after hearing. If free recall were based on processes such as are postulated by the generation-recognition model then one would expect position curves for hearing and enactment which were of differing height but running parallel. Since the serial position curves differ after hearing and enactment, other explanations must be found.

A more complex explanation of the processes in free recall is proposed by Zimmer et al. (1997). In addition to the processes of generation and recognition, they postulate direct accessing to items in free recall. According to this proposal the processes of generation and recognition are, in fact, similar after hearing and enactment, but the direct access makes an important distinction between hearing and enactment. It is only based on item-specific information and uses it directly. Since item-specific information is better after enactment than after hearing, direct access is made greater use of it after enactment. Direct access uses conceptual and motor item-specific information after enactment, accessing the items from the end of the list. This explains why the enactment effect mainly occurs at the rear end of the list. Only when direct access is no longer sufficient do generation and recognition processes become relevant. Since the first items on the list were encoded particularly actively, a primacy effect occurs upon this retrieval.

If the assumption is correct that generation processes do not differ after hearing and enactment and that recognition is better after enactment, then enactment should show retention superiority for the first list items, too. This is often not the case, however. The fact that it is not the case could be due to the fact that episodic-relational information also influences generation. But since the episodic-relational encoding of unrelated actions is poorer after enactment than after hearing, and fewer strategic encoding processes, which produce particularly relational information, are used after enactment, one would, however, expect enactment to be inferior in the primacy effect. The fact that in most cases no differences are to be observed between hearing and enactment in the front part of the serial position curve could be due to the superior item-specific information after enactment, which makes up for the difference in relational information compared with hearing. One should therefore differentiate between categorical-relational and episodic-relational information as two different bases for item generation in recall.

One is forced to make a corresponding differentiation in free recall by the findings on levels of processing. Zimmer and Engelkamp (in press) were able to show convincingly that although no effect of processing depth is shown with short lists, it is with long lists. These and other findings can be explained if a differentiation is made in free recall between reconstruction on the basis of generation and recognition and direct access. If the additional assumption is made that the item-specific information made available by enactment is independent of the instructions for deep processing, then the missing deep-processing effect after enactment with short lists can be explained by the fact that recall is mainly based on direct access of item-specific information. Generation and recognition should only become critical with long lists.

The picture of retrieval processes in free recall has thus been considerably differentiated.

Retrieval Processes in Cued Recall

In cued recall the distinction must be made between paradigms where the cue relates to groups of actions (e.g. presentation of a category) and those where the cue relates to individual actions (e.g. presentation of the object of the action).

Recall of action phrases via a part of a phrase is of theoretical interest because in such a case—especially if the cue relates to the object of the action—it is not possible to refer directly to the action. The word node and concept of a verbal cue are obtained from the cue. From here, verb nodes and action concepts are generated. These must be checked to see if they correspond to an action in the learning episode. The first part of this process, that is the generation of verb nodes and action concepts following a given cue, should occur in the lexicon and in the conceptual system and should not differ after hearing and enactment. The critical difference between hearing and enactment should be in recognition of the generated action concepts. It should be better after enactment than after hearing because only enactment makes motor information available.

Retrieval Processes in Recognition

As with free recall and cued recall, the system approach is useful for explaining performance in recognition and leads to first differentiations of the simple assumption that recognition is primarily due to (undifferentiated) item-specific information. The multimodal theory differentiates after enactment between verbal, conceptual, and motor item-specific encoding components. Considering this differentiation, the question arises as to whether all these components are always involved in recognition.

As the experiments in Chapter 7 have made clear, in recognition after enactment there is neither a level of processing effect (see p. 115) nor a bizarreness effect (Engelkamp et al. 1993; Knopf, 1991). If we presume that instructions for deep processing make additional conceptual item-specific information available, then we must conclude that this is not used in recognition after enactment. From this we can conversely conclude that the recognition after enactment is due to enactment-specific information. Completely analogous conclusions arise on the bizarreness effect in recognition. Without the system differentiation and the selective use of system-specific information in the test, the different performances in recognition after hearing and enactment are difficult to explain.

This picture is added to if we consider the findings on recognition with variable word frequency. Here the lexical or word-node information is varied. It is already known from studies on the purely verbal processing of nouns that frequency of occurrence influences recognition independently of variation of conceptual information. If this holds true, then the lexical information should influence recognition after enactment, too, independently of motor information. According to the findings of Engelkamp et al. (1995), this is the case. In other words, lexical information can be used in recognition after enactment independently of and in addition to conceptual and motor information. This again shows that system differentiation is obviously important and useful for explaining recognition performance.

There is another differentiation of the processes in recognition. It relates to the distinction between automatic and controlled processes (e.g. Gardiner, 1988; Jacoby, 1991). If recognition may be based both on automatic and controlled processes then the question arises as to whether these processes can fall back on information in all the systems or whether controlled and automatic processes make use of the different systems in different ways. This question can be asked from the opposite point of view: Does information from different systems influence automatic and controlled processes to differing degrees? Does information made available in SPTs, for example, have more effect on controlled or automatic processes, and is this information used more by controlled or automatic processes in recognition?

The experiments reported in Chapter 7 have shown that recognition after enactment is primarily controlled and the enactment effect is primarily due to controlled processes. The role of automatic processes is less clear and depends on the theoretical conception of the relationships between automatic and controlled processes (cf. Dehn & Engelkamp, 1997). Either way, the findings support the theory that motor information as made available by enactment is an important basis of conscious recognition processes.

The simple assumption that recognition is basically due to the use of undifferentiated item-specific information has been made complicated in two respects. On the one hand, it is assumed that recognition memory can be based on automatic and controlled processes. On the other hand, different system-specific types of information that can be used in recognition are distinguished (lexical, conceptual, motor).

Retrieval processes with implicit retention

The ideas on implicit retention have also been differentiated by the studies on the enactment effect. It is widely assumed that the distinction must be made in implicit retention between perceptual and conceptual tests (e.g. Engelkamp & Wippich, 1995; Nyberg & Nilsson, 1995; Roediger, 1990). The experiments reported in Chapter 7 make it clear, however, that this differentiation is inadequate. Perceptual tests are characterised by reacting to variations in the physical properties of stimuli. The word identification test is considered to be such a test. Engelkamp et al.'s (1995) findings on word identification have shown, however, that implicit retention performance in this test also reacts to lexical information such as word frequency. This word frequency effect is independent of a change in physical modality (acoustic-visual). This means a perceptual test such as the word identification test also reacts to abstract lexical properties. The multimodal theory is able to take these effects into account by distinguishing concrete, modality-specific, and abstract lexical word nodes (Engelkamp & Zimmer, 1994b, chap. 2).

On the Interplay Between Encoding and Retrieval Processes

Although research into self-performed tasks has made no change to the basic assumption of encoding specificity of retrieval processes or the principle of process overlapping between encoding and retrieval, it makes applying this principle a lot more complicated. This is made especially clear by the fact that in order to predict retention performance it is not enough to separate the encoding conditions of hearing and enactment and to note which test is used. Which processes or which information the specific conditions of the respective encoding situation in the test suggest must also be noted.

These conditions include both specific properties of the material to be learned (e.g. word frequency) and the specific instructions (e.g. with regard to processing depth) in the learning situation. Both aspects can modify the processes in hearing and enactment, in different ways and with different consequences for the different tests. In more concrete terms, not only is there interaction between the encoding condition (hearing, enactment) and the retention test (e.g. free recall, recognition), but also interaction of a higher order which includes factors such as material (e.g. word frequency, list length) or additional encoding instructions (e.g. processing depth).

CHAPTER NINE

Memory for actions and its implications for theories on episodic memory

As far as the development of theories on episodic memory is concerned, the studies on recollection of self-performed actions show that proposals which concentrate too much on individual aspects such as system differentiation (Schacter, 1994) or process differentiation (Roediger, 1990) will eventually not be successful. I believe it is necessary to consider various different aspects and their interplay simultaneously. Two of the process aspects that are actually discussed, and which must be considered hereby, are the differentiation of item-specific and relational information (e.g. Hunt & McDaniel, 1993) and the separation of automatic and controlled processes (e.g. Jacoby, 1991). These process aspects must be considered both in encoding and in retrieval. As the analysis of memory of self-performed actions has shown, these process aspects must be differentiated more strongly than is the case in the current proposals and, more important, these aspects must be considered depending on the systems in which they occur. The system assumptions must be differentiated further, too.

SYSTEMS

With regard to system assumptions it is not enough, for example, to distinguish verbal from visual nonverbal information and both of these again from conceptual information (e.g. Nelson, 1979; Schacter, 1994). A distinction must be made within verbal and nonverbal information between sensory, that is incoming, and motor, that is outgoing, information. Not only that, but sensory and motor information must be more finely differentiated, too.

The study of recollection of self-performed actions has particularly shown that it is necessary to assume not only input systems but also output systems. From a memory psychology point of view, merely perceiving a word is not the same as actually saying it. Analogously, seeing an action is not the same as actually carrying it out. In the multimodal memory theory, therefore, not only were a verbal and a nonverbal input system postulated but also a verbal and a nonverbal output system.

Apart from this, in addition the input systems have to be differentiated further. The differentiation into a verbal and a visual input system, both of which have access to a higher-ranking conceptual system, which is widely accepted (e.g. Ellis & Young, 1989), is not sufficient. The differentiation is taken further in only a few cases, distinguishing in the verbal input system between visual and acoustic word nodes (Schacter, 1994), for example, and in the nonverbal input system between picture nodes and sound nodes (e.g. Riddoch, Humphreys, Coltheart, & Funnell, 1988). Here, too, the study of self-performed actions has led to further differentiations. It became obvious that there is a difference between perceiving a static stimulus (e.g. an object) and a dynamic one (e.g. a movement), two separate sensory systems are involved. Furthermore the motor systems must also be subdivided into subsystems for planning and carrying out an action (cf. also Zimmer & Engelkamp, 1992).

In the usage of the output systems, as in the usage of the input systems, the distinction must also be made as to whether their information becomes activated bottom-up, through stimuli, or top-down, from the conceptual system. On considering the motor systems, an additional point arises. As long as output systems, that is open behaviour, is neglected, concept activation occurs in almost all cases. This is because the stimuli which our attention is focused on are always interpreted semantically. When we perceive an apple we activate its meaning just the same as when we perceive the word "apple". This is not the case with open behaviour. If we take hold of an object, for example our coffee-cup at breakfast, this does not necessarily imply activation of the concept "coffee-cup" and the corresponding awareness of it. With motor behaviour there are direct links from the input to the output side. This direct link should be distinguished from the concept-mediated link between the input and output system (cf. McLeod & Posner, 1984).

If different informational systems are distinguished as in the multimodal memory theory, it becomes obvious that also the assumed processes must be differentiated further.

The study of recollection of self-performed actions has also led to important differentiations in encoding and retrieval processes, which generally have to be taken into consideration in theories of episodic memory. I will first deal with the differentiations in encoding processes.

ENCODING PROCESSES

The study of memory for actions made it clear that in relational encoding one must distinguish between categorical-relational information and episodic-relational information. Both types of relational encoding relate to connections between concepts in the conceptual system. Categorical relational encoding, unlike episodic-relational encoding, uses associations between concepts which already existed before the experiment. This usage usually occurs automatically through activation spreading in the conceptual system upon encoding of the individual items. How the concepts to be learned are accessed (e.g. via linguistic or visual stimuli) should be irrelevant for activation spreading. Categorical-relational encoding should be no different for object concepts with verbal presentation (word lists) and visual presentation (lists of pictures), for example, than for action concepts through hearing or carrying out action phrases.

It is a different situation if new associations are established between concepts which were previously unassociated. Forming new associations in episodic-relational encoding can indeed depend on which systems are involved in encoding and from where the concepts are accessed. Since, for example, carrying out an action restricts information processing to the information that is relevant to the action, it impairs the building of new associations between actions more strongly than the encoding of actions through observation does, which does not specify irrelevant information to such a degree as does carrying out an action. This is why it also tends to allow the coincidentally available context to be included (cf. Engelkamp, 1995b,c).

For this reason it is important that theories of episodic memory distinguish the facility with which certain associations can be established from the facility of the use of associations once they have been established. Only the establishment of new associations varies, dependent on the systems involved in encoding.

Studying memory for actions also showed that the item-specific information must be more strongly differentiated. This differentiation also comes from the distinction between different subsystems. According to the ideas presented here, item-specific information includes all the information which is connected with a concept, especially the information in the input and output systems. With item-specific encoding it is therefore important to bear in mind which other systems or units are activated besides the conceptual system or the concepts. Seeing an apple, for example, activates the corresponding picture node and the concept "apple". But it will not necessarily lead to a naming reaction or to the apple being picked up, that is to the activation of motor programmes. Similarly, being requested to raise one's arm leads to the activation of the word nodes, the action concept, and the motor programme, but not necessarily to the activation of a picture node, such as imagining the action. Item-specific encoding is thus not only determined by the specific task given but also dependent on the systems involved.

This brings us to the pair of terms "automatic" and "controlled" encoding. Before I go on to this, I would like to emphasise once more that the assumptions on item-specific and relational encoding depend on the system assumptions. Thus, relational encoding is limited to the conceptual system whereas item-specific encoding includes all other systems. This is partly due to the fact that free recall starts in the conceptual system. Once a concept has been activated then it can be made more concrete through activation of the nodes and programmes connected with it, and this concretisation permits recognition of the concepts thus activated as being "old".

The distinction between automatic and controlled processes must be considered in any memory theory. It seems to me that the terms "consciousness" and "intent" are of central importance in this distinction, whereby the term "intent" is the narrower of the two. I become conscious of something I wilfully, intentionally direct my attention to. But not everything I register consciously is registered intentionally (cf. Shiffrin & Schneider, 1977). On the other hand, the idea of automatic processes indicates that they are less flexible or variable. They simply take place "automatically". Controlled processes, however, which are subject to the control of the person learning, are more flexible, variable. It is possible to change the focus of attention, direct it towards different things. What is important, as already stated, is that focusing attention on something makes one conscious of that something, but that this can also happen through automatic, that is not wilfully controlled, processes. However, this situation is made more complicated by the fact that automatic processes normally run in the context of controlled processes.

Again these differentiations become obvious in considering the performance of actions. If one is asked to tear up a sheet of paper, this action will be initiated wilfully, whereas the processes involved in the actual motor performance of the action run automatically. Not every partial movement is carried out under wilful control. In this respect performance of the action is strategy-free, as Cohen (e.g. 1985) postulated. However, performing the action leads to more awareness in encoding than does the processing involved in hearing action phrases. This is partly due to the fact that learning action phrases through hearing does not greatly concretise the action concepts through modality-specific information; carrying out the action, on the other hand, forces such concretisation. This seems to support the further assumption that conscious processes are connected with item-specific rather than relational information.

All this is extremely speculative. Hardly any empirical studies have tried to measure these aspects in encoding directly, but those that have are important for considering the retrieval processes. Interestingly, the distinction between automatic and controlled processes is discussed more in connection with retrieval processes (e.g. Jacoby, 1991; Jacoby & Dallas, 1981; Mandler, 1980; Richardson-Klavehn & Gardiner, 1995) than with processes in encoding (e.g. Hasher & Zacks, 1979). What is discussed even less, however, is the interplay of automatic and controlled processes in encoding and retrieval. Yet it is imperative for any theory of explicit recall to explicitly consider this distinction between processes in encoding and retrieval.

RETRIEVAL PROCESSES

Retrieval processes have become more differentiated through studying memory for actions. The differentiation of the processes in free recall is the most important for theories of episodic memory in general. It is not enough to distinguish between generation and recognition in free recall. Certain items are apparently recalled by means of direct access. It is assumed that this direct access is based on good item-specific information. It has been emphasised repeatedly that carrying out actions makes such item-specific information available automatically. The direct access is expressed in an extended, marked recency effect. It is interesting to investigate whether other stimuli or tasks also promote direct access.

The considerations on cued recall have opened a completely new perspective on recall processes. The processes underlying cued recall are usually considered to be similar to those underlying free recall. In a way, it is free recall supported by cues. On analysis of the findings on recollection of self-performed actions, however, it became apparent that one important difference between free recall and cued recall—at least when the cues are verbal in nature—can be that cued recall is not started in the conceptual system, like free recall, but in the lexicon. This is at least true of cued recall of phrases or sentences where a word of the phrases or sentences acts as the cue. In these cases, a phrase or sentence is generated on a linguistic level. Only then is a check carried out on a conceptual level—and, in the case of actions performed, on the basis of motor information too—to decide if the generated item belongs to the learning episode. The general conclusion from this idea is that one must consider which system is first activated by the respectively selected cues. Which further systems become relevant in recall and the order in which this happens may depend on this.

In recognition memory, two processes have been distinguished since the early 1980s (Jacoby & Dallas, 1981; Mandler, 1980): Recognition can either be retrieval-based, or controlled, or it can be familiarity-based, or automatic. In this context the further distinction between intentionality and consciousness in recognition has recently been discussed (Mecklenbräuker, 1995; Richardson-Klavehn & Gardiner, 1995; Wippich, 1992). This is partly due to the fact that precisely this distinction is neglected in the process-dissociation approach as proposed by Jacoby (1991). It therefore seems desirable to start up two distinctions: one between conscious and unconscious and the other between intentional and nonintentional. I have also proposed such a distinction and added an assumption that otherwise normally remains implicit if it is made at all: Conscious recall and recognition require conscious encoding.

Another new assumption concerning recognition memory is that the information used in a recognition test may also depend on the types of information encoded at study. Word frequency and type of encoding (here: hearing vs. enactment), for example, proved to be independent factors of word frequency; encoding condition on recognition indicates that words of varying frequency make different lexical information available; and besides conceptual information, self-performance makes motor information available that is missing in hearing.

Altogether, these considerations on retrieval show that one must not only take into account which different processes can be used in the different test methods, but also which types of information, that is which subsystems, are used there. This is also the case for implicit retention tests, which I have only touched on here.

Altogether, the conclusion is that memory theories must look at which memory traces are laid down upon encoding and how they are sought and discriminated upon recall. In the effort to solve these problems no memory theory will be able to avoid making system differentiations and explaining what the encoding and retrieval processes are and how they depend on the systems involved.

CHAPTER TEN

Widening the perspective

Central to this book is the question of why we remember so well actions we have performed ourselves. The actions considered were simple actions such as "to wash one's hands", "to hang up the overcoat", "to close the door", "to fold up the shirt", etc. The "good" memory for self-performed actions was mainly demonstrated by contrasting it with memory for such actions that one has observed of other people, or that one has only heard about, which is less good than memory for self-performed actions. The interesting point of the good memory for self-performed actions is that it is good even if the actions are unrelated. In everyday life, many simple actions occur in meaningfully linked sequences, such as when we repair a chair. Such sequences of actions are linked in a meaningful structure to achieve a goal. Memory of such action sequences is of course dependent on the pre-experimental knowledge structure of such sequences. However, memory for such organised action sequences was not the topic of this book. Here, I focused on the stimulating phenomenon that we remember actions very well, even when they are unrelated. Such memory is also to be found in everyday life, for instance, when someone is asking us questions such as "have you already posted the letter", "watered the flowers", "bought the bread", "washed your hair", etc. This good memory for unrelated actions is biologically functional. It prevents, for instance, repeating things we have already done, and which we do not want to repeat, such as paying the waiter for the meal twice. However, there are also situations in which this good memory for self-performed actions breaks down. In previous chapters I have said almost nothing about such situations. Situations in which we fail to remember self-performed actions in everyday life will be discussed in this final chapter.

In a further section, I will contrast retrospective remembering of self-performed actions—as discussed in the bulk of this book—with prospective memory of actions. Prospective memory refers to memory for actions that we intend to perform after a certain time has elapsed. To discuss this contrast seems particularly desirable because there are almost no relationships in the literature between these two fields of research. The experimental paradigms as well as the theoretical explanations differ in both domains.

FAILURES OF REMEMBERING SELF-PERFORMED ACTIONS

It has already been mentioned that remembering one's own actions is functional and biologically important. It would be disastrous if we paid a bill repeatedly or congratulated a person repeatedly because we had forgotten that we had already paid or congratulated. The evolution has protected us against such failures in that we remember our actions almost automatically when necessary. I have discussed a series of aspects, demonstrating how this protection works. Among these aspects was the one that enactment guarantees within certain frame conditions a processing of information that makes the memory trace of the enacted action highly distinctive. An important frame condition is the fact that performing the actions is conceptually mediated. Self-performing does not lead *per se* to a good memory trace, but only when conceptually mediated.

In the following paragraphs, I will discuss three types of failure to remember self-performed actions, which are in a sense the price for good memory in normal cases. With these failures, I will demonstrate how the features of processing self-performed actions that usually provide good memory foster memory failures under specific conditions.

As mentioned, it is a central function of our memory for self-performed actions to prevent us repeating the enactment unintentionally. The most important mechanism in this context is the ability to recognise that we have already performed an action (e.g. having already watered the flowers). This means, more important than the ability to remember actions in free recall is the ability to recognise that we have already performed an action, for instance, when someone is asking us: "Have you already watered the flowers?" or when we form anew the intention to water the flowers. For this reason, recognition memory for self-performed actions is extremely good.

This recognition memory is explicit. We remember the first enactment consciously. Therefore, this mechanism only functions when we have planned and executed the action consciously. Because conscious planning and executing actions is time-consuming, it does not come as a surprise that have mechanisms also evolved that enable us to enact actions without awareness. This automatic triggering of motor reactions to associated stimuli is phylogenetically older than conscious enactment. In this case, enactment is based on pre-existing connections between action programmes and triggering conditions (Neumann & Prinz, 1987). Such direct stimulus-response associations are, for instance, given when experienced drivers drive a car. Using the clutch, the accelerator, the brake occur automatically with experienced drivers. In everyday life, we plan and execute actions on certain levels consciously and do not so on other levels. For instance, we decide, usually consciously, to take the road map out of the car. Within this global action, part actions may occur automatically (e.g. to unlock the car, open the glove compartment, take out the road map, close the glove compartment, lock the car, etc.). The latter actions are under direct stimulus control. Such automatizations unburden us. However, a consequence may be that we do not remember whether we performed part actions or not. Someone who has just taken the road map out of his or her car may ask himself, for instance, whether he or she has locked the car. Generally speaking, the probability that we do not remember a part action (such as: Did I lock the car? Did I put sugar into the tea? etc.) is the greater the more stimulus-controlled the action was. The more a global action becomes a routine, the worse is our explicit memory of the part actions. In such case, it may be necessary to check whether an action was indeed performed. A meaningful technique to protect oneself against such memory failures is to make efforts to perform consciously such actions that one would like to remember. Whether such efforts are justified—that is, whether the possibly necessary check is more disturbing than the effort to perform the action consciously—must be decided by each person for him- or herself. It may be mentioned that the process of checking whether one has already performed an action is not based on the same mechanisms for healthy persons as it is for persons with compulsion who are driven to check again and again whether they have performed certain actions (Ecker, 1995).

Another type of failure to remember self-performed actions can be observed particularly with increasing age: telling people things twice (Koriat, Ben-Zur, & Sheffer, 1988). This failure depends on the particular features of encoding by enactment. It became repeatedly clear in the course of the book that enactment focuses information processing on the action-relevant pieces of information. A consequence of this focusing is that context processing is neglected insofar as the context is irrelevant for the action proper. When a story teller is repeatedly telling the same stories, it may be his or her goal to entertain the audience. For reporting the story, it is often unimportant who the audience is, so this fact is not action-relevant, and therefore, it is not encoded at telling the story. So, the story teller knows that he or she has already told the story, and probably also knows that he or she has told the story repeatedly (this should be the case due to the good item-specific encoding of self-performed actions), but remembers less well to whom he or she has already told the story (for the very same feature of encoding by enactment). Indeed Koriat et al. (1991) have experimentally demonstrated that participants remember better that they had learned an action after SPT than after EPT encoding, but they remembered better in which room they had seen or performed an action after EPT than after SPT encoding. It is therefore the downside of the good item-specific encoding of SPTs which is beneficial for remembering the action itself that the context of the action is poorly encoded and consequently poorly remembered. In order to avoid such failures as the repeated telling of the same story to the same people, it seems worthwhile to consider when telling the story why one tells the story to this particular person.

The third failure of memory I would like to point out is also a consequence of the specific feature of encoding by enactment. This failure is reflected in the title of a paper of Rita Anderson (1984): "Did I do it or did I only imagine it?" We can experience difficulty in deciding whether we have performed an action or whether we have only intended to perform the action, but then for what reason ever have not performed it. I have demonstrated that one can induce such failures in experiments, when I asked participants to perform actions immediately, while simultaneously to plan to perform them again later. Memory for the actions was worse under these conditions than when the actions were only performed immediately (Engelkamp, 1997). An explanation for this effect can be seen in the overlapping encoding processes under both conditions (immediate performance and intention to perform later). The similarity of the encoding processes impairs their discrimination.

A similar situation is given when one imagines to self-perform an action and when one actually performs the action. These two conditions lead to similar and overlapping encoding processes, which impair their discrimination in memory. This impairment was demonstrated experimentally by Ecker and Engelkamp (1995). They requested their subjects (1) to perform actions, (2) to imagine how they self-performed actions, (3) to imagine how someone else performed actions, and (4) to repeat the verbal descriptions of the actions. In a later recognition memory test, the subjects were not only requested to indicate whether a presented action was old or new, but also to indicate for the "old" actions whether they had performed, imagined self-performing, imagined other performing, or verbally repeated the action phrase in the study situation. It was observed that confusions arose more often between self-performing and imagining self-performing (cf. Goff & Roediger, 1998, for similar findings).

There is little that one can do against such confusions. The processing overlap is not easy to reduce. However, it should be noted that the absolute frequency of confusion was low in the experiment between even self-performance and imagining self-performance. Positively formulated, one can state that memory for the manner of encoding is very good even if the kind of encoding is highly similar.

RETROSPECTIVE VERSUS PROSPECTIVE
MEMORY OF ACTIONS

Prospective memory means remembering actions that one intended to perform in the future. This memory is different from retrospective memory for actions, that is for actions one has performed at study. I have already discussed briefly prospective memory in Chapter 5, where I tried to separate the effects of planning and execution in retrospective memory of actions and where I tried to demonstrate that the action planning, which is an inherent part of every conceptually mediated enactment of actions, can only explain part of the enactment effect. I will return here once more to prospective memory of actions because it is studied independently of retrospective memory of actions in spite of its close relationship to it. It may therefore be useful to elaborate a little similarities and differences between both.

We invariably intend to perform certain actions in the course of a day, and it is not unusual that we forget to perform some of these actions. The necessity to remember actions prospectively exists for single actions as well as for series of actions. In both cases, the necessity to remember the actions prospectively results from the fact that the actions can not or should not be performed immediately. For example, when one wants to wish someone happy birthday, one must wait for the corresponding day before one can congratulate. The necessity to remember several actions emerges from the fact that one cannot perform them simultaneously. It might be our intention to have our hair cut, submit our tax return to the revenue office, make an appointment with a friend by telephone, repair a broken window, etc. In order to be able to perform such a series of actions, we must bring them into a sequence. In doing so, the importance and urgency of the single actions has to be considered (Dörner, 1986). In order to bring the actions into a sequence and to perform them successively, we are forced to keep our intentions to perform the actions and the action concepts themselves activated. After we have ordered them, we must remember to perform them at an appropriate time. I will deal briefly with both aspects.

When we remember single actions, it is important to distinguish whether an external cue is triggering our memory to perform the intended action (event-based prospective memory) or whether there is no such an external cue, but the action must be performed at a certain point in time (time-based prospective memory; McDaniel & Einstein, 1992). Time-based prospective memory is, for instance, given when we want to bring the plants into the house in the evening in order to protect them against the coldness of the night. Event-based prospective memory is, for instance, given when passing a letter box reminds us to post a letter.

First, time-based prospective memory of single actions was studied. For this purpose, the to-be-remembered actions were embedded in other experiments without making the purpose of the prospective memory test obvious for the subjects. The experimenter requested the subjects, for instance, to post a letter for him or to call him or her a given time after the experiment (Harris, 1983; Meacham & Singer, 1977; West, 1988). However, this "ecological" paradigm to study prospective memory has the disadvantage that one can scarcely control the various factors that might influence the performance level (from external cues to strategies of rehearsal). For this reason, Einstein and McDaniel (1990) developed a laboratory paradigm, which allows study of prospective memory under better controlled conditions. The introduction of this paradigm implicated at the same time a shift from the study of time-based to event-based prospective memory.

The core idea of Einstein and McDaniel (1990) was to give the subjects a dual task so that the prospective memory task was embedded in another task. This other task was a short-term memory task. For this task, subjects are visually presented with short sequences of words, which they have to recall immediately. Before the short-term memory tasks are started, they are instructed for the prospective memory task. They are told that, during the short-term memory task, they have to press a key whenever one of three words (e.g. cup, star, boat) appears. Prospective memory is measured by counting how frequently a subject reacts to the three target words.

One of the central questions studied in this context was the role of the type of the cue words (targets) in remembering the desired reaction (key press). It turned out that the familiarity of the targets (familiar targets were more often overlooked than unfamiliar targets), as well as the distinctivity of the targets (a target word is more efficient when it appears in the context of different words than when it appears in the context of similar words), influenced prospective memory performance (Brandimonte & Passolunghi, 1994; Einstein & McDaniel, 1990; Mäntylä, 1993; McDaniel & Einstein, 1993; Passolunghi, Brandimonte, & Cornoldi, 1995).

Event-based prospective memory can be divided into two components. First, the cue word must be recognised as such. The subject must become aware of the fact that the word, e.g. "boat", is meant to remind him or her to perform an action. Second, the subject must remember what action he or she intended to perform. In the study of Einstein and McDaniel (1990), for instance, the subject had to remember to press a key when the target showed up. Distinctivity and familiarity serve primarily the first function, that is to recognise the cue as a cue. For the second function, that is to remember the corresponding action to the cue, the association between cue and action is important. The second function has received little attention in the field of prospective memory research. From the perspective of retrospective memory of actions, this situation comes as a surprise.

The study of retrospective memory of actions has made it clear that actions are most efficiently cued by cue words that are an inherent part of the denoted actions (Engelkamp & Perrig, 1986). In this sense, the cue "window" is more efficient after enacting the phrase "to throw the apple out of the window" than after enacting the phrase "to eat the apple at the window". This effect was explained by assuming that encoding by enacting leads to focusing upon action-relevant information while, at the same time, ignoring action-irrelevant information. In other words, enactment integrates action-relevant information particularly well. This action-integrating function of enactment should also become efficient when an action is planned or its performance intended for prospective memory, although possibly to a more minor extent.

If these considerations hold true, event-based prospective memory should be enhanced (1) if action-inherent features are used as cues, and (2) if care is taken that the link between action and cue is already encoded. According to the latter assumption, it is not sufficient when at encoding only an abstract connection between cue and action (e.g. between the word "boat" and key pressing) is realised (as it is the case when subjects only hear about this connection), and it is even less sufficient when in the encoding instructions attention is primarily directed to the cue word.

That in planning to perform an action in response to a cue the cue–action relationship is important seems to be self-evident and trivial. Nevertheless, this aspect is largely ignored if cues are used in experiments that have no "natural" relationship to the reactions (such as "boat"–key press).

In this context, the research of retrospective memory of action phrases has made clear that action-inherent cues (e.g. the objects of action) are more efficient the more strongly the label of objects and their corresponding actions are associated. In this sense, the word "book" is more efficient for the phrase "to read the book" than for the phrase "to lift the book". In addition to this pre-experimental object–verb association, cued recall is further enhanced when the action is enacted or planned rather than when only the action phrase is listened to (e.g. Engelkamp, et al., 1993).

It is self-evident that in everyday life it is not always possible to use the objects of actions as cues for prospective memory. Nevertheless, one should use the objects as cues wherever it is possible. In this sense, it is better to use the letter itself as a cue rather than a knot in your handkerchief if you want to remind yourself to post a letter.

In sum, from this discussion of retrospective memory of actions it follows for event-based prospective memory that not only is the encoding of the cues important but also the encoding of the cue-action relationship. It should be an advantage when (1) the cue is an inherent part of the to-be-remembered action, (2) the cue and the action are associated pre-experimentally, and (3) in the study phase the cue–action relationship is not only encoded on an abstract (conceptual) level, but also as planning the action as a response to the cue on a concrete (modality-specific) level. In order to achieve this goal, the cue–action relationship, including the enactment of the action, must be focused upon during the instruction phrase.

With regard to the relationship between event-based prospective memory and retrospective memory of actions, it can be concluded:

1. The fact that prospective memory research has focused on rather arbitrary cues for the to-be-remembered actions and on the specific properties of such cues has disguised rather than enlightened the relationship between the research of prospective and retrospective memory of actions.
2. The encoding of the cue–action relationship in prospective memory is clearly related to the study of this process in retrospective memory of actions. However, until now this aspect has received little attention in the study of prospective memory. It is desirable that this aspect receives more attention in future research of prospective memory.
3. It is surprising that the research of prospective memory has been restricted to the prospective memory of single actions, although it is an everyday requirement that we remember series of planned actions, for instance, when we plan to go shopping or when we plan what we want to do in the course of a day. Remembering to perform a series of intended actions has more similarities with remembering a series of performed actions than has remembering a single action prospectively. It is therefore to be wished that prospectively memory of a series of actions should receive more attention in the future.

References

Anderson, J.R. (1985). *Cognitive psychology and its implications*. New York: Freeman.

Anderson, J.R., & Bower, G.H. (1972). Recognition and retrieval processes in free recall. *Psychological Review, 79*, 97–123.

Anderson, M.C., Bjork, R.A., & Bjork, E.L. (1994). Remembering can cause forgetting: Retrieval dynamics in long-term memory. *Journal of Experimental Psychology: Learning, Memory, and Cognition, 20*, 1063–1087.

Anderson, R.E. (1984). Did I do it or did I only imagine doing it? *Journal of Experimental Psychology: General, 113*, 594–613.

Atkinson, R.C., & Shiffrin, R.M. (1968). Human memory: A proposed system and its control processes. In K.W. Spence & J.T. Spence (Eds.), *The psychology of learning and motivation: Advances in research and theory* (Vol. 2). New York: Academic Press.

Bäckman, L. (1985). Further evidence for the lack of adult age differences on free recall of subject-performed tasks: The importance of motor action. *Human Learning, 4*, 79–87.

Bäckman, L., & Nilsson, L.-G. (1984). Aging effects in free recall: An exception to the rule. *Human Learning, 3*, 53–69.

Bäckman, L., & Nilsson, L.-G. (1985). Prerequisites for lack of age differences in memory performance. *Experimental Aging Research, 11*, 67–73.

Bäckman, L., Nilsson, L.G., & Chalom, D. (1986). New evidence on the nature of the encoding of action events. *Memory and Cognition, 14*, 339–346.

Bäckman, L., Nilsson, L.-G., Herlitz, A., Nyberg, L. & Stigsdotter, A. (1991). A dual conception of the encoding of action events. *Scandinavian Journal of Psychology, 32*, 289-299.

Bäckman, L., Nilsson, L.G., & Kormi-Nouri, R. (1993). Attentional demands and recall of verbal and color information in action events. *Scandinavian Journal of Psychology, 34*, 246–254.

Baddeley, A.D. (1986). *Working memory*. Oxford: University Press.

Baddeley, A.D., & Hitch, G.J. (1974). Working memory. In G.A. Bower (Ed.), *The psychology of learning and motivation* (Vol. 8). New York: Academic Press.

Bahrick, H.P. (1970). Two-phase model for prompted recall. *Psychological Review, 77*, 215–222.

Bahrick, H.P., & Boucher, B. (1968). Retention of visual and verbal codes of the same stimuli. *Journal of Experimental Psychology, 78*, 417–422.

Bäuml, K.H. (1996). Revisiting an old issue: Retroactive interference as a function of the degree of original and interpolated learning. *Psychonomic Bulletin and Review, 3*, 380–384.

Begg, I. (1978). Imagery and organization in memory: Instructional effects. *Memory and Cognition, 6*, 174–183.

Begg, I. (1983). Imagery instructions and the organization of memory. In J.C. Yuille (Ed.), *Imagery, memory and cognition*. Hillsdale, NJ.: Lawrence Erlbaum Associates Inc.

Bjork, R.A. (1972). Theoretical implications of directed forgetting. In A.W. Melton & E. Martin (Eds.), *Coding processes in human memory*. Washington DC: Winston.

Boles, D.B. (1983). Dissociated imageability, concreteness, and familiarity in lateralized word recognition. *Memory and Cognition, 11*, 511–519.

Bower, G.H. (1970). Imagery as a relational organizer in associative learning. *Journal of Verbal Learning and Verbal Behavior, 8*, 323–343.

Bower, G.H. (1972). Mental imagery and associative learning. In L.W. Gregg (Ed.), *Cognition in learning and memory*. New York: Wiley.

Brandimonte, M.A., & Passolunghi, M.C. (1994). The effect of cue-familiarity, cue-distinctiveness, and retention interval on prospective remembering. *Quarterly Journal of Experimental Psychology, 47A*, 565–587.

Brooks, B.M., & Gardiner, J.M. (1994). Age differences in memory for prospective compared with retrospective subject-performed tasks. *Memory and Cognition, 22*, 27–33.

Clark, H.H., & Carlson, T.B. (1981). Context for comprehension. In J. Long & A. Baddeley (Eds.), *Attention and performance IX*. Hillsdale, NJ: Lawrence Erlbaum Associates Inc.

Cohen, R.L. (1981). On the generality of some memory laws. *Scandinavian Journal of Psychology, 22*, 267–281.

Cohen, R.L. (1983). The effect of encoding variables on the free recall of words and action events. *Memory and Cognition, 11*, 575–582.

Cohen, R.L. (1985). On the generality of the laws of memory. In L.G. Nilsson & T. Archer (Eds.), *Animal learning and human memory*. Hillsdale, NJ: Lawrence Erlbaum Associates Inc.

Cohen, R.L. (1989a). Memory for action events: The power of enactment. *Educational Psychological Review, 1*, 57–80.

Cohen, R.L. (1989b). The effects of interference tasks on recency in the free recall of action events. *Psychological Research, 51*, 176–180.

Cohen, R.L., & Bean, G. (1983). Memory in educable mentally retarded adults: Deficit in subject or experimenter. *Intelligence, 7*, 287–298.

Cohen, R.L., & Bryant, S. (1991). The role of duration in memory and meta-memory of enacted instructions (SPTs). *Psychological Research, 53*, 183–187.

Cohen, R.L., & Heath, M. (1988). Recall probabilities for enacted instructions. In M.M. Gruneberg, P.E. Morris, & R.N. Sykes (Eds.), *Practical aspects of memory: Current research and issues* (Vol. 1). Chichester, UK: Wiley.

Cohen, R.L., Peterson, M., & Mantini-Atkinson, T. (1987). Interevent differences in event memory: Why are some events more recallable than others? *Memory and Cognition, 15*, 109–118.

Cohen, R.L., Sandler, S.P., & Schroeder, K. (1987). Aging and memory for words and action events: Effects of item repetition and list length. *Psychology and Aging, 2*, 280–285.

Cohen, R.L., & Stewart, M. (1982). How to avoid developmental effects in free recall. *Scandinavian Journal of Psychology, 23*, 9–16.

Cornoldi, C., Corti, M.T., & Helstrup, T. (1994). Do you remember what you imagined you would do in that place? The motor encoding cue-failure effect in sighted and blind people. *Quarterly Journal of Experimental Psychology, 47A*, 311–329.

Cornoldi, C., & De Beni, R. (1986). Retrieval times in the usage of concrete and abstract mnemonic cues associated to loci. In D.G. Russell, D.F. Marks & J.T.E. Richardson (Eds.), *Imagery 2*. Dunedin, New Zealand: Human Performance Associates.

Craik, F.I.M., & Jennings, J.M. (1992). Human memory. In F.I.M. Craik & T.A. Salthouse (Eds.), *The handbook of aging and cognition*. Hillsdale, NJ: Lawrence Erlbaum Associates Inc.

Craik, F.I.M., & Lockhart, R.S. (1972). Levels of processing: A framework for memory research. *Journal of Verbal Learning and Verbal Behavior, 11*, 671–684.

Craik, F.I.M., & Tulving, E. (1975). Depth of processing and the retention of words in episodic memory. *Journal of Experimental Psychology: General, 104*, 268–294.

De Renzi, E., Faglioni, P., & Sorgato, P. (1982). Modality-specific and supramodal mechanisms of apraxia. *Brain, 105*, 301–312.

Dehn, D., & Engelkamp, J. (1997). Process dissociation procedure: Double dissociations following divided attention and speeded responding. *Quarterly Journal of Experimental Psychology: Human Experimental Psychology, 50A*, 318–336.

Denis, M., Engelkamp, J., & Mohr, G. (1991). Memory of imagined actions: Imagining oneself or another person. *Psychological Research, 53*, 246–250.

Dick, M.B., Kean, M.L., & Sands, D. (1989). Memory for action events in Alzheimer-type dementia: Further evidence of an encoding failure. *Brain and Cognition, 9*, 71–87.

Dörner, D. (1986). Intention memory and intention regulation. In F. Klix & H. Hagendorf (Eds.), *Human memory and cognitive capabilities: Mechanisms and performances, Part B*. Amsterdam: Elsevier.

Ecker, W. (1995). *Kontrollzwänge und Handlungsgedächtnis*. Regensburg, Germany: S. Roderer.

Ecker, W., & Engelkamp, J. (1995). Memory for actions in obsessive-compulsive disorder. *Behavioural and Cognitive Psychotherapy, 23*, 349–371.

Eich, J.E. (1980). The cue-dependent nature of state-dependent retrieval. *Memory and Cognition, 8*, 57–63.

Einstein, G.O., & Hunt, R.R. (1980). Levels of processing and organization: Additive effects of individual item and relational processing. *Journal of Experimental Psychology: Learning, Memory, and Cognition, 10*, 133–143.

Einstein, G.O., & McDaniel, M.A. (1987). Distinctiveness and the mnemonic benefits of bizarre imagery. In M.A. McDaniel & M. Pressley (Eds.), *Imagery and related mnemonic processes*. New York: Springer.

Einstein, G.O., & McDaniel, M.A. (1990). Normal aging and prospective memory. *Journal of Experimental Psychology: Learning, Memory, and Cognition, 16*, 717–726.

Ellis, A.W., & Young, A.W. (1989). *Human cognitive neurospychology*. Hove, UK: Lawrence Erlbaum Associates Ltd.

Engelkamp, J. (1985). Aktivationsprozesse im motorischen Gedächtnis. In D. Albert (Ed.), *Bericht über den 34. Kongreß der Deutschen Gesellschaft für Psychologie in Wien*. Göttingen, Germany: Hogrefe.

Engelkamp, J. (1986a). Differences between imaginal and motor encoding. In F. Klix & H. Hagendorf (Eds.), *Human memory and cognitive capabilities*. Amsterdam: Elsevier (North-Holland).

Engelkamp, J. (1986b). Nouns and verbs in paired-associate learning: Instructional effects. *Psychological Research, 48*, 153–159.

Engelkamp, J. (1988). Modality-specific encoding and word class in verbal learning. In M. Gruneberg, P.E. Morris, & R.N. Sykes (Eds.), *Practical aspects of memory: Current research and issues* (Vol. 1). Chichester, UK: Wiley.

Engelkamp, J. (1989). Memory for performed and imaged noun pairs and verb pairs: A comment on Tore Helstrup. *Psychological Research, 50*, 241–242.

Engelkamp, J. (1990). *Das menschliche Gedächtnis*. Göttingen, Germany: Hogrefe.

Engelkamp, J. (1991a). Imagery and enactment in paired-associate learning. In R. H. Logie & M. Denis (Eds.), *Mental images in human cognition*. Amsterdam: Elsevier.

Engelkamp, J. (1991b). Memory of action events: Some implications for memory theory and for imagery. In C. Cornoldi & M. McDaniel (Eds.), *Imagery and cognition*. New York: Springer.

Engelkamp, J. (1994). Episodisches Gedächtnis: Von Speichern zu Prozessen und Informationen. *Psychologische Rundschau, 45*, 195–210.

Engelkamp, J. (1995a). Explaining retention: Lines of development and problems. In B. Boothe, R. Hirsig, A. Helminger, B. Meier, & R. Volkart (Eds.), *Perception—evaluation—interpretation*. Bern, Switzerland: Hogrefe & Huber.

Engelkamp, J. (1995b). Visual imagery and enactment of actions in memory. *British Journal of Psychology, 86*, 227–240.

Engelkamp, J. (1995c). Zum visuellen Erkennen von Objekten und Wörtern. *Sprache & Kognition, 14*, 174–192.

Engelkamp, J. (1997). Memory for to-be-performed tasks versus memory for performed tasks. *Memory and Cognition, 25*, 117–124.

Engelkamp, J., Biegelmann, U., & McDaniel, M.A. (1998). Relational and item-specific information: Trade-off and redundancy. *Memory, 6*, 307–333.

Engelkamp, J., & Cohen, R.L. (1991). Current issues in memory of action events. *Psychological Research, 53*, 175–182.

Engelkamp, J., & Dehn, D. (1997). Strategy and consciousness in remembering subject-performed actions. *Sprache & Kognition, 16*, 94–109.

Engelkamp, J., & Krumnacker, H. (1980). Imaginale und motorische Prozesse beim Behalten verbalen Materials. *Zeitschrift für experimentelle und angewandte Psychologie, 27*, 511–533.

Engelkamp, J., Mohr, G., & Zimmer, H.D. (1991). Pair-relational encoding of performed nouns and verbs. *Psychological Research, 53*, 232–239.

Engelkamp, J., & Perrig, W. (1986). Differential effects of imaginal and motor encoding on the recall of action phrases. *Archiv für Psychologie, 138*, 261–273.

Engelkamp, J., & Wippich, W. (1995). Current issues in implicit and explicit memory. *Psychological Research, 57*, 143–155.

Engelkamp J., & Zimmer, H.D. (1983). Zum Einfluß von Wahrnehmen und Tun auf das Behalten von Verb-Objekt-Phrasen. *Sprache & Kognition, 2*, 117–127.

Engelkamp, J., & Zimmer, H.D. (1984). Motor program information as a separable memory unit. *Psychological Research, 46*, 283–299.

Engelkamp, J., & Zimmer, H.D. (1985). Motor programs and their relation to semantic memory. *German Journal of Psychology, 9*, 239–254.

Engelkamp, J., & Zimmer, H.D. (1989). Memory for action events: A new field of research. *Psychological Research, 51*, 153–157.

Engelkamp, J., & Zimmer, H.D. (1994a). Motor similarity in subject-performed tasks. *Psychological Research, 57*, 47–53.

Engelkamp, J., & Zimmer, H.D. (1994b). *The human memory: A multi-modal approach*. Seattle, WA: Hogrefe & Huber.

Engelkamp, J., & Zimmer, H.D. (1995). Similarity of movement in recognition of self-performed tasks. *British Journal of Psychology, 86*, 241–252.

Engelkamp, J., & Zimmer, H.D. (1996). Organization and recall in verbal tasks and in subject-performed tasks. *European Journal of Cognitive Psychology, 8*, 257–273.

Engelkamp, J., & Zimmer, H.D. (1997). Sensory factors in memory for subject-performed tasks. *Acta Psychologica, 96*, 43–60.

Engelkamp, J., Zimmer, H.D., & Biegelmann, U. (1993). Bizarreness effects in verbal tasks and subject-performed tasks. *European Journal of Cognitive Psychology, 5*, 393–415.

Engelkamp, J., Zimmer, H.D., & Denis, M. (1989). Paired-associate learning of action verbs with visual- or motor-imaginal encoding instructions. *Psychological Research, 50*, 257–263.

Engelkamp, J., Zimmer, H.D., & Kurbjuweit, A. (1995). Verb frequency and enactment in implicit and explicit memory. *Psychological Research, 57*, 242–249.

Engelkamp, J., Zimmer, H.D., & Mohr, G. (1990). Differential memory effects of concrete nouns and action verbs. *Zeitschrift für Psychologie, 198*, 189–216.

Engelkamp, J., Zimmer, H.D., Mohr, G., & Sellen, O. (1994). Memory of self-performed tasks: Self-performing during recognition. *Memory and Cognition, 22*, 34–39.

Fendrich, D.M., Healy, A.F., & Bourne, L.E., Jr. (1991). Long-term repetition effects for motoric and perceptual procedures. *Journal of Experimental Psychology: Learning, Memory, and Cognition, 17*, 137–163.

Foley, M.A., Bouffard, V., Raag, T., & Di Santo-Rose, M. (1991). The effects of enactive encoding, type of movement, and imagined perspective on memory of dance. *Psychological Research, 53*, 251–259.

Forbach, G., Stanners, R., & Hochhaus, L. (1974). Repetition and practice effects in a lexical decision task. *Memory and Cognition, 2*, 337–339.

Gardiner, J.M. (1988). Functional aspects of recollective experience. *Memory and Cognition, 16*, 309–313.

Gardiner, J.M., Gregg, V.H., & Hampton, J.A. (1988). Word frequency and generation effects. *Journal of Experimental Psychology: Learning, Memory, and Cognition, 14*, 687–693.

Garnham, A. (1985). *Psycholinguistics*. London: Methuen.

Gillund, G., & Shiffrin, R.M. (1984). A retrieval model for both recognition and recall. *Psychological Review, 91*, 1–67.

Glanzer, M., & Cunitz, A.R. (1966). Two storage mechanisms in free recall. *Journal of Verbal Learning and Verbal Behavior, 5*, 351–360.

Glanzer, M., & Schwartz, A. (1971). Mnemonic structure in free recall: Differential effects on STS and LTS. *Journal of Verbal Learning and Verbal Behavior, 10*, 194–198.

Glass, A.L., Millen, D.R., Beck, L.J., & Eddy, J.K. (1985). Representation of images in sentence verification. *Journal of Memory and Language, 24*, 442–466.

Godden, D., & Baddeley, A.D. (1975). Context-dependent memory in two natural environments: On land and under water. *British Journal of Psychology, 66*, 325–331.

Godden, D., & Baddeley, A.D. (1980). When does context influence recognition memory? *British Journal of Psychology, 71*, 99–104.

Goff, L.M., & Roediger, H.L., III. (1998). Imagination inflation for action events: Repeated imaginings lead to illusory recollections. *Memory and Cognition, 26*, 20–33.

Gorman, A.M. (1961). Recognition memory for nouns as a function of abstractness and frequency. *Journal of Experimental Psychology, 61*, 23–29.

Graf, P., & Komatsu, S. (1994). Process dissociation procedure: Handle with caution. *European Journal of Cognitive Psychology, 6*, 113–129.

Graf, P., & Mandler, G. (1984). Activation makes words more accessible, but not necessarily more retrievable. *Journal of Verbal Learning and Verbal Behavior, 23*, 553–568.

Harley, W. (1965). The effect of monetary incentive in paired associate learning using a differential method. *Psychonomic Science, 2*, 377–378.

Harris, J.E. (1983). Remembering to do things: A forgotten topic. In J.E. Harris & P.E. Morris (Eds.), *Everyday memory, actions, and absent mindedness*. New York: Academic Press.

Hasher, L., & Zacks, R.T. (1979). Automatic and effortful processes in memory. *Journal of Experimental Psychology: General, 108*, 556–588.

Heilman, K.M. (1973). Ideational apraxia—a re-definition. *Brain, 96*, 861–864.

Helstrup, T. (1986). Separate memory laws for recall of performed acts? *Scandinavian Journal of Psychology, 27*, 1–29.

Helstrup, T. (1987). One, two or three memories? A problem-solving approach to memory for performed acts. *Acta Psychologica, 66,* 37–68.

Helstrup, T. (1989a). Loci for act recall: Contextual influence on processing of action events. *Psychological Research, 51,* 168–175.

Helstrup, T. (1989b). Memory for performed and imaged noun pairs and verb pairs. *Psychological Research, 50,* 237–240.

Helstrup, T. (1991). Integration versus nonintegration of noun pairs and verb pairs under enactment and nonenactment conditions. *Psychological Research, 53,* 240–245.

Helstrup, T. (1993). Inter-event differences in action memory. *Scandinavian Journal of Psychology, 34,* 328–337.

Helstrup, T., & Molander, B. (1996). Procedural dependence in action memory: Effects of verb form and individual vs. group conditions. *Scandinavian Journal of Psychology, 37,* 329–337.

Heuer, H. (1985). Some points of contact between models of central capacity and factor analytic models. *Acta Psychologica, 60,* 135–155.

Heuer, H., & Schmidtke, V. (1996). Secondary-task effects on sequence learning. *Psychological Research, 59,* 119–133.

Higbee, K.L. (1977). *Your memory, how it works and how to improve it.* Englewood Cliffs, NJ: Prentice-Hall.

Hines, D. (1976). Recognition of verbs, abstract nouns, and concrete nouns from the left and right visual half-fields. *Neuropsychologia, 14,* 211–216.

Hirshman, E., & Bjork, R.A. (1988). The generation effect: Support for a two-factor theory. *Journal of Experimental Psychology: Learning, Memory, and Cognition, 14,* 484–494.

Hoffmann, J. (1993). *Vorhersage und Erkenntnis.* Göttingen: Hogrefe.

Homa, D., & Viera, C. (1988). Long-term memory for pictures under conditions of thematically related foils. *Memory and Cognition, 16,* 411–421.

Humphreys, G.W., Evett, J.L., Quinlan, P.T., & Besner, D. (1987). Orthographic priming: Qualitative differences between priming from identified and unidentified primes. In M. Coltheart (Ed.), *Attention and performance: XII. The psychology of reading.* Hove, UK: Lawrence Erlbaum Associates Ltd.

Hunt, R.R., & Einstein, G.O. (1981). Relational and item-specific information in memory. *Journal of Verbal Learning and Verbal Behavior, 20,* 497–514.

Hunt, R.R., & McDaniel, M.A. (1993). The enigma of organization and distinctiveness. *Journal of Memory and Language, 32,* 421–445.

Hunt, R.R., & Seta, C.E. (1984). Category size effects in recall: The roles of relational and individual item information. *Journal of Experimental Psychology, 10,* 454–464.

Hyde, T.S., & Jenkins, J.J. (1969). The differential effects of incidental tasks on the organization of recall of a list of highly associated words. *Journal of Experimental Psychology, 82,* 472–481.

Jacoby, L.L. (1983). Perceptual enhancement: Persistent effects of an experience. *Journal of Experimental Psychology: Learning, Memory, and Cognition, 9,* 21–38.

Jacoby, L.L. (1991). A process dissociation framework: Separating automatic from intentional uses of memory. *Journal of Memory and Language, 30,* 513–541.

Jacoby, L.L., & Dallas, M. (1981). On the relationship between autobiographical memory and perceptual learning. *Journal of Experimental Psychology: General, 110,* 306–340.

Jacoby, L.L., Toth, J.P., Yonelinas, A.P., & Debner, J.A. (1994). The relationship between conscious and unconscious influences: Independence or redundancy. *Journal of Experimental Psychology: General, 123,* 216–219.

Johnson, P. (1982). The functional equivalence of imagery and movement. *Quarterly Journal of Psychology, 34A,* 349–365.

Kausler, D.H. (1982). *Experimental psychology and human aging.* New York: Wiley.

Kausler, D.H. (1989). Impairment in normal memory aging: Implications of laboratory evidence. In G.C. Gilmore, P.J. Whitehouse, & M.L. Wykle (Eds.), *Memory aging and dementia*. New York: Springer.

Kausler, D.H. (1994). *Learning and memory in normal aging*. New York: Academic Press.

Kausler, D.H., Lichty, W., & Davis, R.T. (1985). Temporal memory for performed activities: Intentionality and adult age differences. *Developmental Psychology*, *21*, 1132–1138.

Kausler, D.H., Lichty, W., & Freund, J.S. (1985). Adult age differences in recognition memory and frequency judgments for planned activities. *Developmental Psychology*, *21*, 647–654.

Kausler, D.H., Lichty, W., Hakami, M.K., & Freund, J.S. (1986). Activity duration and adult age differences in memory for activity performance. *Journal of the Psychology of Aging*, *1*, 80–81.

Kinoshita, S. (1989). Masked and unmasked repetition effects: Activation of representation or procedure? In S. Lewandowski, J.C. Dunn, & K. Kirsner (Eds.), *Implicit memory: Theoretical issues* (pp. 213–227). Hillsdale, NJ: Lawrence Erlbaum Associates Inc.

Kintsch, W. (1968). Recognition and free recall of organized lists. *Journal of Experimental Psychology*, *78*, 481–487.

Kintsch, W. (1970). Models for free recall and recognition. In D.A. Norman (Ed.), *Models of human memory*. New York: Academic Press.

Knopf, M. (1989). *Lernen und Behalten von Handlungen im höheren Erwachsenenalter—Die Rolle von Vertrautheit und Aufgabenschwierigkeit*. München, Germany: Max-Planck Institut für Psychologische Forschung.

Knopf, M. (1991)..Having shaved a kiwi fruit: Memory of unfamiliar subject-performed actions. *Psychological Research*, *53*, 203–211.

Knopf, M. (1992). *Gedächtnis für Handlungen: Funktionsweise und Entwicklung*. Heidelberg, Germany: Habilitationsschrift, Universität Heidelberg.

Knopf, M. (1995). Das Erinnern eigener Handlungen im Alter. *Zeitschrift für Psychologie*, *203*, 335–349.

Knopf, M., & Neidhardt, E. (1989). Gedächtnis für Handlungen unterschiedlicher Vertrautheit—Hinweise aus entwicklungspsychologischen Studien. *Sprache & Kognition*, *8*, 203–215.

Koriat, A., Ben-Zur, H., & Druch, A. (1991). The contextualisation of input and output events in memory. *Psychological Research*, *53*, 260–270.

Koriat, A., Ben-Zur, H., & Nussbaum, A. (1990). Encoding information for future action: Memory for to-be-performed versus memory for to-be-recalled tasks. *Memory and Cognition*, *18*, 568–578.

Koriat, A., Ben-Zur, H., & Sheffer, D. (1988). Telling the same story twice: Output monitoring and age. *Journal of Memory and Language*, *27*, 23–39.

Kormi-Nouri, R. (1994). *Memory for action events: An episodic integration view*. Unpublished doctoral dissertation, Umeå University, Sweden.

Kormi-Nouri, R. (1995). The nature of memory for action events: An episodic integration view. *European Journal of Cognitive Psychology*, *7*, 337–363.

Kormi-Nouri, R., Nilsson, L.-G., & Bäckman, L. (1994). The dual conception view reexamined: Attentional demands and the encoding of verbal and physical information in action events. *Psychological Research*, *57*, 42–46.

Kormi-Nouri, R., Nyberg, L., & Nilsson, L.-G. (1994). The effect of retrieval enactment on recall of self-performed tasks and verbal tasks. *Memory and Cognition*, *22*, 723–728.

Lichty, W., Bressie, S., & Krell, R. (1988). When a fork is not a fork: Recall of performed activities as a function of age, generation, and bizarreness. In M.M. Gruneberg, P.E. Morris, & R.N. Sykes (Eds.), *Practical aspects of memory: Current research and issues* (Vol. 1). Chichester, UK: Wiley.

Lichty, W., Kausler, D.H., & Martinez, D.R. (1986). Adult age differences in memory for motor versus cognitive activities. *Experimental Aging Research, 12,* 227–330.

Lockhart, R.S., & Craik, F.I.M. (1990). Levels of processing: A retrospective commentary on a framework of memory research. *Canadian Journal of Psychology, 44,* 87–112.

Lockhart, R.S., Craik, F.I.M., & Jacoby, L.L. (1976). Depth of processing, recognition and recall: Some aspects of a general memory system. In J. Brown (Ed.), *Recall and recognition.* London: Wiley.

Logie, R.H. (1991). Visuo-spatial short-term memory: Visual working memory or visual buffer. In C. Cornoldi & M.A. McDaniel (Eds.), *Imagery and cognition.* Berlin, Germany: Springer.

Logie, R.H. (1995). *Visuo-spatial working memory.* Hove, UK: Lawrence Erlbaum Associates Ltd.

Lupker, S.J. (1988). Picture naming: An investigation of the nature of categorical priming. *Journal of Experimental Psychology: Learning, Memory, and Cognition, 14,* 444–455.

Madigan, S. (1983). Picture memory. In J.C. Yuille (Ed.), *Imagery, memory and cognition.* Hillsdale, NJ: Lawrence Erlbaum Associates Inc.

Mandler, G. (1967). Organization and memory. In K.W. Spence & J.T. Spence (Eds.), *The psychology of learning and motivation* (Vol. 1). New York: Academic Press.

Mandler, G. (1968). Association and organization: Facts, fancies, and theories. In T.R. Dixon & D.L. Horton (Eds.), *Verbal behavior and general behavior theory.* Englewood Cliffs, NJ: Prentice-Hall.

Mandler, G. (1980). Recognizing: The judgement of previous occurrence. *Psychological Review, 87,* 252–271.

Mandler, G., Goodman, G.O., & Wilkes-Gibbs, D.L. (1982). The word-frequency paradox in recognition. *Memory and Cognition, 10,* 33–42.

Mäntylä, T. (1993). Knowing but not remembering: Adult age differences in recollective experience. *Memory and Cognition, 21,* 379–388.

Marschark, M., & Hunt, R.R. (1989). A reexamination of the role of imagery in learning and memory. *Journal of Experimental Psychology: Learning, Memory, and Cognition, 15,* 710–720.

Marschark, M., & Surian, L. (1989). Why does imagery improve memory? *European Journal of Cognitive Psychology, 1,* 251–263.

McClelland, J.L., & Rumelhart, D.E. (1981). An interactive activation model of context effects in letter perception: Pt. 1. An account of basic findings. *Psychological Review, 88,* 375–407.

McDaniel, M.A., & Einstein, G.O. (1992). Aging and prospective memory: Basic findings and practical applications. In T.E. Scruggs & M.A. Mastropieri (Eds.), *Advances in learning and behavioral disabilities* (Vol. 8). Greenwich, C.T: JAI Press.

McDaniel, M.A., & Einstein, G.O. (1993). The importance of cue familiarity and cue distinctiveness in prospective memory. *Memory, 1,* 23–41.

McDaniel, M.A., Einstein, G.O., Dunay, P.K., & Cobb, R.E. (1986). Encoding difficulty and memory: Toward a unifying theory. *Journal of Memory and Language, 25,* 645–656.

McDaniel, M.A., Einstein, G.O., & Lollis, T. (1988). Qualitative and quantitative considerations in encoding difficulty effect. *Memory and Cognition, 16,* 8–14.

McDaniel, M.A., Waddill, P.J., & Einstein, G.O. (1988). A contextual account of the generation effect: A three-factor theory. *Journal of Memory and Language, 27,* 521–536.

McLeod, P., & Posner, M.I. (1984). Privileged loops from percept to act. In H. Bouma & D.G. Bouwhuis (Eds.), *Attention and performance X: Control of language processes.* Hove, UK: Lawrence Erlbaum Associates Ltd.

Meacham, J.A., & Singer, J. (1977). Incentive effects in prospective remembering. *Journal of Psychology, 97,* 191–197.

Mecklenbräuker, S. (1995). Input and output monitoring in implicit and explicit memory. *Psychological Research, 57,* 179–191.

Meltzoff, A.N. (1988). Infant imitation after a 1-week delay: Long-term memory for novel acts and multiple stimuli. *Developmental Psychology, 24*, 470–476.

Meltzoff, A.N. (1990). Foundations for developing a concept of self: The role of imitation in relating self to other and the value of social mirroring, social modeling, and self practice in infancy. In D. Cicchetti & M. Beeghly (Eds.), *The self in transition: Infancy to childhood*. Chicago: University of Chicago Press.

Meyer, D.E., & Schvaneveldt, R.W. (1971). Facilitation in recognizing pairs of words: Evidence of a dependence between retrieval operations. *Journal of Experimental Psychology, 90*, 227–234.

Mohr, G. (1992). Retrieval of action phrases: The efficacy of verb cues and noun cues. *Zeitschrift für Psychologie, 200*, 363–370.

Mohr, G., Engelkamp, J., & Zimmer, H.D. (1989). Recall and recognition of self-performed acts. *Psychological Research, 51*, 181–187.

Murdock, B.B. (1960). The immediate retention of unrelated words. *Journal of Experimental Psychology, 60*, 222–234.

Nairne, J.S., Riegler, G.L., & Serra, M. (1991). Dissociative effects of generation on item and order retention. *Journal of Experimental Psychology: Learning, Memory, and Cognition, 17*, 702–709.

Naveh-Benjamin, M. (1987). Coding of spatial location information: An automatic process? *Journal of Experimental Psychology: Learning, Memory, and Cognition, 13*, 595–605.

Navon, O., & Gopher, D. (1979). On the economy of the human processing system. *Psychological Review, 86*, 214–255.

Nelson, D.L. (1979). Remembering pictures and words: Appearance, significance and name. In L. Cermak & F.I.M. Craik (Eds.), *Levels of processing in human memory*. Hillsdale, NJ: Lawrence Erlbaum Associates Inc.

Nelson, T.O., Metzler, J., & Reed, D. (1974). Role of details in the long-term recognition of pictures and verbal descriptions. *Journal of Experimental Psychology, 102*, 184–186.

Neumann, O. (1992). Theorien der Aufmerksamkeit: Von Metaphern und Mechanismen. *Psychologische Rundschau, 43*, 83–101.

Neumann, O. & Prinz, W. (1987). Kognitive Antezedenzien von Willkürhandlungen [Cognitive antecendents of voluntary actions]. In H. Heckhausen, P.M. Gollwitzer, & F.E. Weinert (Eds.), *Jenseits des Rubikon: Der Wille in den Humanwissenschaften*. Berlin, Germany Springer.

Nilsson, L.G., & Cohen, R.L. (1988). Enrichment and generation in the recall of enacted and non-enacted instructions. In M.M. Gruneberg, P.E. Morris, & R.N. Sykes (Eds.), *Practical aspects of memory: Current research and issues* (Vol. 1). Chichester, UK, Wiley.

Nilsson, L.G., Cohen, R.L., & Nyberg, L. (1989). Recall of enacted and nonenacted instructions compared: Forgetting functions. *Psychological Research, 51*, 188–193.

Nilsson, L.G., & Craik, F.I.M. (1990). Additive and interactive effects in memory for subject-performed tasks. *European Journal of Cognitive Psychology, 2*, 305–324.

Norman, D.A., & Bobrow, D. (1975). On data-limited and resource-limited processing. *Cognitive Psychology, 7*, 44–64.

Norris, M., & West, R. (1991). Age differences in the recall of actions and cognitive activities: The effects of presentation rate and object cues. *Psychological Research, 53*, 188–194.

Norris, M., & West, R. (1993). Activity memory and aging: The role of motor retrieval and strategic processing. *Psychology and Aging, 8*, 81–86.

Nyberg, L. (1993). *The enactment effect: Studies of memory phenomenon*. Unpublished doctoral dissertation, University of Umeå, Sweden.

Nyberg, L., & Nilsson, L.-G. (1995). The role of enactment in implicit and explicit memory. *Psychological Research, 57*, 215–219.

Nyberg, L., Nilsson, L.G., & Bäckman, L. (1991). A component analysis of action events. *Psychological Research, 53*, 219–225.

Ochipa, C., Mothi, L.J.G., & Heilman, K.M. (1990). Conduction apraxia. *Journal of Clinical and Experimental Neuropsychology, 12,* 89.

Oesterreich, R., & Ködding, C. (1995). Das Generieren von Handlungsvor-stellungen im Modell "Netz erinnerbaren Handelns" und der Tu-Effekt. *Zeitschrift für experimentelle Psychologie, 42,* 280–301.

Oloffson, U. (1996). The effect of enactment on memory for order. *Psychological Research, 59,* 75–79.

Paivio, A. (1969). Mental imagery in associative learning and memory. *Psychological Review, 76,* 241–263.

Paivio, A. (1971). *Imagery and verbal processes.* New York: Holt, Rinehart, & Winston.

Paivio, A. (1986). *Mental representations: A dual coding approach.* New York: Oxford University Press.

Paivio, A., & Olver, M. (1964). Denotative-generality, imagery, and meaningfulness in paired-associate learning of nouns. *Psychonomic Science, 1,* 183–184.

Passolunghi, M.C., Brandimonte, M.A., & Cornoldi, C. (1995). Encoding modality and prospective memory in children. *International Journal of Behavioral Development, 18,* 631–648.

Perrig, W., & Hofer, D. (1989). Sensory and conceptual representations in memory: Memory images that cannot be imaged. *Psychological Research, 51,* 201–207.

Prinz, W. (1987). Ideo-motor action. In H. Heuer & A.F. Sanders (Eds.), *Perspectives on perception and action.* Hillsdale, NJ: Lawrence Erlbaum Associates Inc.

Raaijmakers, J.G.W., & Shiffrin, R.M. (1981). Search of associative memory. *Psychological Review, 88,* 93–134.

Rabinowitz, J.C., Mandler, G., & Barsalou, L.W. (1979). Generation-recognition as an auxiliary retrieval strategy. *Journal of Verbal Learning and Verbal Behavior, 18,* 57–72.

Ratner, H.H., & Hill, L. (1991). The development of children's action memory. When do actions speak louder than words? *Psychological Research, 53,* 195–202.

Richardson-Klavehn, A., & Gardiner, J.M. (1995). Retrieval volition and memorial awareness in stem completion: An empirical analysis. *Psychological Research, 57,* 166–178.

Riddoch, M.J., Humphreys, G.W., & Price, C.J. (1989). Routes to action: Evidence from apraxia. *Cognitive Neuropsychology, 6,* 437–454.

Riddoch, M.J., Humphreys, G.W., Coltheart, M., & Funnell, E. (1988). Semantic systems or system? Neuropsychological evidence re-examined. *Cognitive Neuropsychology, 5,* 3–25.

Roediger, H.L. (1990). Implicit memory. *American Psychologist, 45,* 1045–1056.

Roediger, H.L., Weldon, M.S., Stadler, M.L., & Riegler, G.L. (1992). Direct comparison of two implicit memory tests: Word fragment and word stem completion. *Journal of Experimental Psychology: Learning, Memory, and Cognition, 18,* 1251–1269.

Roenker, D.L., Thompson, C.P., & Brown, S.C. (1971). Comparison of measures for the estimation of clustering in free recall. *Psychological Bulletin, 76,* 45–48.

Rothi, L.J.G., Ochipa, C., & Heilman, K.M. (1991). A cognitive neuropsychological model of limb praxis. *Cognitive Neuropsychology, 8,* 443–458.

Rundus, D. (1971). Analysis of rehearsal processes in free recall. *Journal of Experimental Psychology, 89,* 63–77.

Saltz, E. (1988). The role of motoric enactment (M-processing) in memory for words and sentences. In M.M. Gruneberg, P.E. Morris, & R.N. Sykes (Eds.), *Practical aspects of memory: Current research and issues* (Vol. 1). Chichester, UK: Wiley.

Saltz, E., & Dixon, D. (1982). Let's pretend: The role of motoric imagery in memory for sentences and words. *Journal of Experimental Child Psychology, 34,* 77–92.

Saltz, E., & Donnenwerth-Nolan, S. (1981). Does motoric imagery facilitate memory for sentences? A selective interference test. *Journal of Verbal Learning and Verbal Behavior, 20,* 322–332.

Schaaf, M.G. (1988). Motorische Aktivität und verbale Lernleistung—Leistungssteigerung durch Simultanität? *Zeitschrift für experimentelle und angewandte Psychologie, 35,* 298–302.

Schacter, D.L. (1994). Priming and multiple memory systems: Perceptual mechanisms of implicit memory. In D.L. Schacter & E. Tulving (Eds.), *Memory systems 1994.* Cambridge, MA: MIT Press.

Schneider, W., & Shiffrin, R.M. (1977). Controlled and automatic human information processing: I. Detection, search and attention. *Psychological Review, 84,* 1–66.

Serra, M., & Nairne, J.S. (1993). Design controversies and the generation effect: Support for an item-order hypothesis. *Memory and Cognition, 21,* 34–40.

Shanon, B. (1979). Lateralization effects in response to words and nonwords. *Cortex, 15,* 541–549.

Shiffrin, R.M., & Atkinson, R.C. (1969). Storage and retrieval processes in long-term memory. *Psychological Review, 76,* 179–193.

Shiffrin, R.M. & Schneider, W. (1977). Controlled and automatic human information processing: II. Perceptual learning, automatic attending and general theory. *Psychological Review, 84,* 127–190.

Slamecka, N.J., & Katsaiti, L.T. (1987). The generation effect as an artifact of selective displaced rehearsal. *Journal of Memory and Language, 26,* 589–607.

Smith, S.M., Glenberg, A., & Bjork, R.A. (1979). Environmental context and human memory. *Memory and Cognition, 6,* 342–353.

Smyth, M.M., Morris, P.E., Levy, P., & Ellis, A.W. (1987). *Cognition in action.* Hove, UK: Lawrence Erlbaum Associates Ltd.

Snodgrass, J.G. (1984). Concepts and their surface representation. *Journal of Verbal Learning and Verbal Behavior, 23,* 3–22.

Strack, E., & Bless, H. (1994). Memory for non-occurrences: Metacognitive and presuppositional strategies. *Journal of Memory and Language, 33,* 203–217.

Svensson, T., & Nilsson, L.G. (1989). The relationship between recognition and cued recall in memory of enacted and nonenacted information. *Psychological Research, 51,* 194–200.

Tulving, E. (1985). How many memory systems are there? *American Psychologist, 40,* 385–398.

Tulving, E., & Psotka, J. (1971). Retroactive inhibition in free recall: Inaccessibility of information available in the memory store. *Journal of Experimental Psychology, 87,* 1–8.

Tulving, E., & Thomson, D.M. (1973). Encoding specificity and retrieval processes in episodic memory. *Psychological Review, 80,* 352–373.

Wessels, M.G. (1984). *Kognitive Psychologie.* New York: Harper & Row.

West, R.L. (1988). Prospective memory and aging. In M.M. Gruneberg, P.E. Morris, & R.N. Sykes (Eds.), *Practical aspects of memory: Current research and issues* (Vol. 2). London: Academic Press.

Wippich, W. (1981). Duale Kode-Theorie und die Konzeption der Analysestufen. *Semiotik, 3,* 294–310.

Wippich, W. (1990a). Begreifen oder Fühlen? Motorische und sensorische Prozesse bei Erinnerungen an haptische Informationen. *Archiv für Psychologie, 142,* 181–193.

Wippich, W. (1990b). Erinnerungen an Gerüche: Benennungsmaße und autobiographische Erinnerungen zeigen Geruchsnachwirkungen an. *Zeitschrift für experimentelle und angewandte Psychologie, 37,* 679–695.

Wippich, W. (1991). Haptic information processing in direct and indirect memory tests. *Psychological Research, 53,* 162–168.

Wippich, W. (1992). Implicit and explicit memory without awareness. *Psychological Research, 54,* 212–224.

Wippich, W., & Wagner, V. (1989). Auch Hände haben ein Gedächtnis. *Sprache & Kognition, 8,* 166–177.

Zimmer, H.D. (1984). *Enkodierung, Rekodierung, Retrieval und die Aktivation motorischer Programme* (Arbeiten der FR Psychologie Nr. 91). Saarbrücken, Germany: Universität des Saarlandes.

Zimmer, H.D. (1988). Formkonzepte und Bildmarken: Zwei verschiedene Repräsentationen für visuell-sensorische Merkmale? *Sprache & Kognition, 7,* 40–50.

Zimmer, H.D. (1991). Memory after motoric encoding in a generation-recognition model. *Psychological Research, 53,* 226–231.

Zimmer, H.D. (1992). *No LOP-effects with subject-performed tasks? They are here.* Paper presented at the 5th conference of the ESCOP, Paris.

Zimmer, H.D. (1994). Representation and processing of the spatial layout of objects with verbal and nonverbal input. In W. Schnotz & R. Kulhavy (Eds.), *Comprehension of graphics.* Amsterdam: Elsevier.

Zimmer, H.D. (1995a). Memory for spatial location and enactment. *Psychologische Beiträge, 38,* 404–417.

Zimmer, H.D. (1995b). Size and orientation of objects in explicit and implicit memory: A reversal of the dissociation between perceptual similarity and type of test. *Psychological Research, 57,* 260–273.

Zimmer, H.D., & Engelkamp, J. (1984). Planungs- und Ausführungsanteile motorischer Gedächtniskomponenten und ihre Wirkung auf das Behalten ihrer verbalen Bezeichnungen. *Zeitschrift für Psychologie, 192,* 379–402.

Zimmer, H.D., & Engelkamp, J. (1985). An attempt to distinguish between kinematic and motor memory components. *Acta Psychologica, 58,* 81–106.

Zimmer, H.D., & Engelkamp, J. (1989a). Does motor encoding enhance relational information? *Psychological Research, 51,* 158–167.

Zimmer, H.D., & Engelkamp, J. (1989b). One, two or three memories: Some comments and new findings. *Acta Psychologica, 70,* 293–304.

Zimmer, H.D., & Engelkamp, J. (1992). *Gedächtnispsychologische Aspekte der Planung, Wahrnehmung und Ausführung von Handlungen* (Arbeiten der Fachrichtung Psychologie Nr. 171). Saarbrücken, Germany: Universität des Saarlandes.

Zimmer, H.D., & Engelkamp, J. (1996). Routes to actions and their efficacy for remembering. *Memory, 4,* 59–78.

Zimmer, H.D., & Engelkamp, J. (in press). Levels-of-processing effects in subject-performed tasks. *Memory and Cognition.*

Zimmer, H.D., Engelkamp, J., & Sieloff, U. (1984). Motorische Gedächtniskomponenten als partiell unabhängige Komponenten des Engramms verbaler Handlungsbeschreibungen. *Sprache & Kognition, 3,* 70–85.

Zimmer, H.D., Engelkamp, J., Mohr, M., & Mohr, G. (1988). *Organisation und Behalten im multimodalen Modell* (Arbeiten der Fachrichtung Psychologie Nr. 125). Saarbrücken, Germany: Universität des Saarlandes.

Zimmer, H.D., Helstrup, T., Engelkamp, J., & Saathoff, J. (1997). Pop-out into memory: A supplementary retrieval mechanism for subject-performed tasks. Unpublished manuscript.

Author Index

Subject Index